DESPERATELY SEEKING WARHOL

IAN CASTELLO-CORTES

GINGKO PRESS

BEGINNINGS

Andy Warhol, who more than any other artist seemed to define the very zeitgeist of the USA, was also a living embodiment of the American dream. From a poor, Ruthenian (Slovak) Catholic family in the heavily industrialised city of Pittsburgh, he quickly, almost instinctively, scaled the heights of New York's commercial art world. By the age of 27 he was one of the highest paid and most fashionable fashion illustrators in the City.

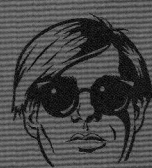

Andy's Wigs

From an early age, Andy was incredibly self-conscious about his appearance, the result of his blotchy skin and a bulbous nose due to his St Vitus's Dance condition. When he started going bald in the 1950s, Andy decided to resort to wigs – he could use them not just to look cool, but, brilliantly, particularly with his silver wig, to turn himself into easily the most recognised artist in the USA. Before he went out, in the evening, Andy would carefully prepare his skin and attach and shape his chosen wig, a process he described as "glueing". In time Andy would own over 400 wigs.

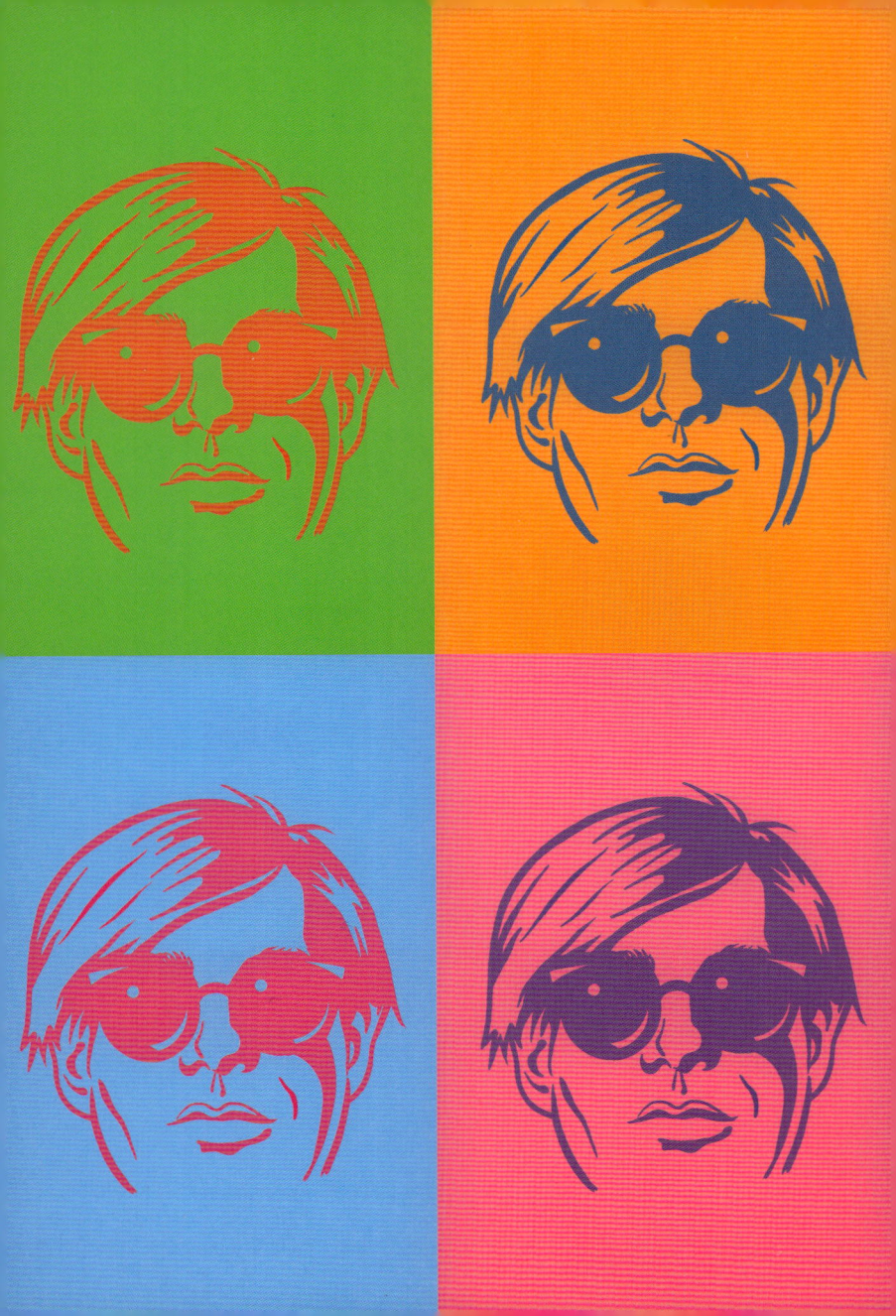

1

MIKOVÁ

"I come from nowhere."
Andy Warhol

Andy Warhol was a living paradox. When asked where he came from, it was either "nowhere" or "Pittsburgh," and yet he remained true to the faith into which he was born all his life – a sect of Byzantine Catholicism from where the Warholas (Andy later dropped the last 'a') hailed, Mikova in Slovakia, close to the Hungarian and Ukrainian border. Andy's parents emigrated to Pittsburgh in the 1920s, and maintained close ties with the Ruthenian community there. Andy's dad, Ondrej, was a road-layer and builder. His mother, Julia, spoke no English, and the Warholas spoke their particular Slovakian dialect at home. Their social life revolved around the Church, to which they happily walked six miles every Sunday. A more provincial and less auspicious background for the future king of pop art is hard to imagine.

WHERE?
CHURCH IN MIKOVA, OF WOODEN CONSTRUCTION
WITH TRADITIONAL 'ONION' SPIRE.
SLOVAKIA.

(2)

3252 DAWSON STREET

"We're not Hungarian. We're not Slovak. We're not Ukrainian."
One of the Warholas' neighbours in Pittsburgh.

When the Warholas arrived in the USA, they were close to the bottom rung of the social ladder. But Ondrej was a grafter and a saver. Heavily industrial Pittsburgh was booming in the 1920s and there was plenty of work. When Andy, the youngest of three boys, was born on August 6th, 1928, the Warholas lived in a modest 'row house' in the Soho slum neighbourhood. When the depression struck, Ondrej lost his job but had enough savings to see his family through. Julia worked as a cleaner for a few dollars a week. Extreme thrift was the order of the day, but unlike many families in Pittsburgh, they weren't reliant on soup kitchens. After the depression, Ondrej got his old job back and had saved enough to buy the Warholas' first house, at 3252 Dawson Street, in the Oakland neighborhood, for cash, in 1933. The house was near the Holmes School, which Andy attended from the second grade. Ondrej was determined that at least one of his sons should go to college – he would lift his family out of poverty.

WHERE?
OAKLAND NEIGHBOURHOOD,
PITTSBURGH.

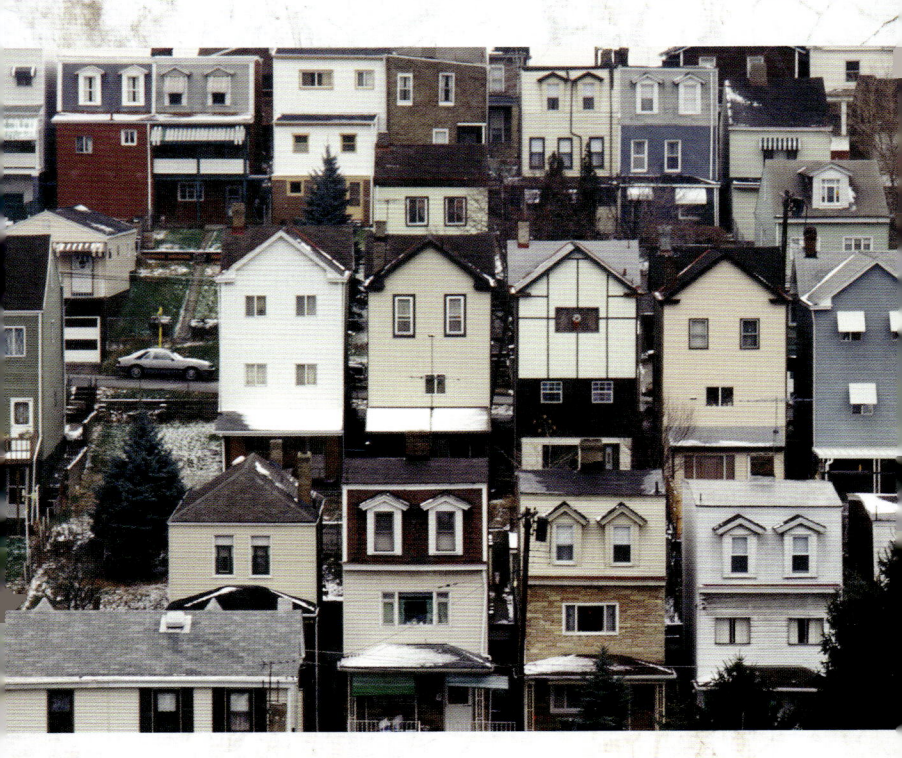

3

ST VITUS'S DANCE

"When I was little...I learned that you actually have more power when you shut up." **Andy Warhol**

As a child Andy was a bit feeble and accident-prone, but it was contracting St Vitus's Dance (chorea) at the age of eight that defined his childhood. His case was mild, but with enough shaking in his hands and slurring of speech to worry Julia sick. Their close relationship – she devoted herself to his constant care and bought him comics, movie magazines and colouring books – intensified. He stayed in bed for a month before being forced back to school, suffered a relapse, and went back to bed, drawing and dreaming for a further four weeks. Julia was warned that he could suffer further relapses, and became very protective. Andy was treated like the special child. He also developed the blotchy skin condition that would plague him for the rest of his life. Yet something had gelled in those eight weeks of being at home, a certain confidence, a detachment from the common herd and an ability to manipulate those around him.

WHAT?
AS A BOY, ANDY LOVED DICK TRACY CARTOONS.
WHEN ILL, DICK TRACY WAS A COMFORTING COMPANION.
LATER ANDY WOULD MAKE THE CHARACTER ONE OF HIS
FIRST FORAYS INTO POP ART.

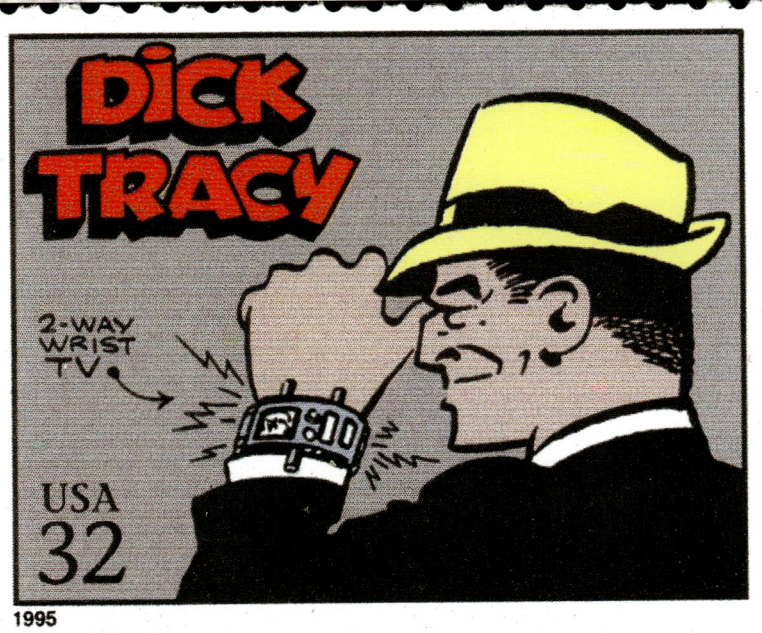

4

CARNEGIE INSTITUTE

"A more talented person than Andy Warhol I never knew."
Joseph Fitzpatrick, Carnegie Museum.

If you had talent, Pittsburgh was full of opportunity. Andy's talent was recognised by Annie Vickermann, his brilliant art teacher at the Holmes School, when he was nine. She recommended him for a Saturday course at the Carnegie Museum. Then, at Schenley High School, Andy revealed a compulsive, obsessive streak when it came to his art, drawing endlessly, paying no attention to other students. Ondrej's death at the age of 57 was a disaster for the Warholas, but Andy bounced back when he was accepted on the prestigious Carnegie Institute art course. Usually the preserve of Pittsburgh's elite, he was able to attend thanks to Ondrej's savings. Andy thrived at Carnegie, winning the Leisser prize. It was here that he also developed his distinctive and fast blotted-line drawing technique, which would become the mainstay of his commercial art career. Andy was already breaking down barriers between commercial art and fine art. He put it to good use when he was hired, whilst still a student, by art director Larry Vollmer to do window backdrops for the upscale Pittsburgh department store, Joseph Horne. Andy now set his sights on New York.

WHERE?
THE CAMPUS AT CARNEGIE INSTITUTE
(NOW PART OF CARNEGIE-MELLON UNIVERSITY).

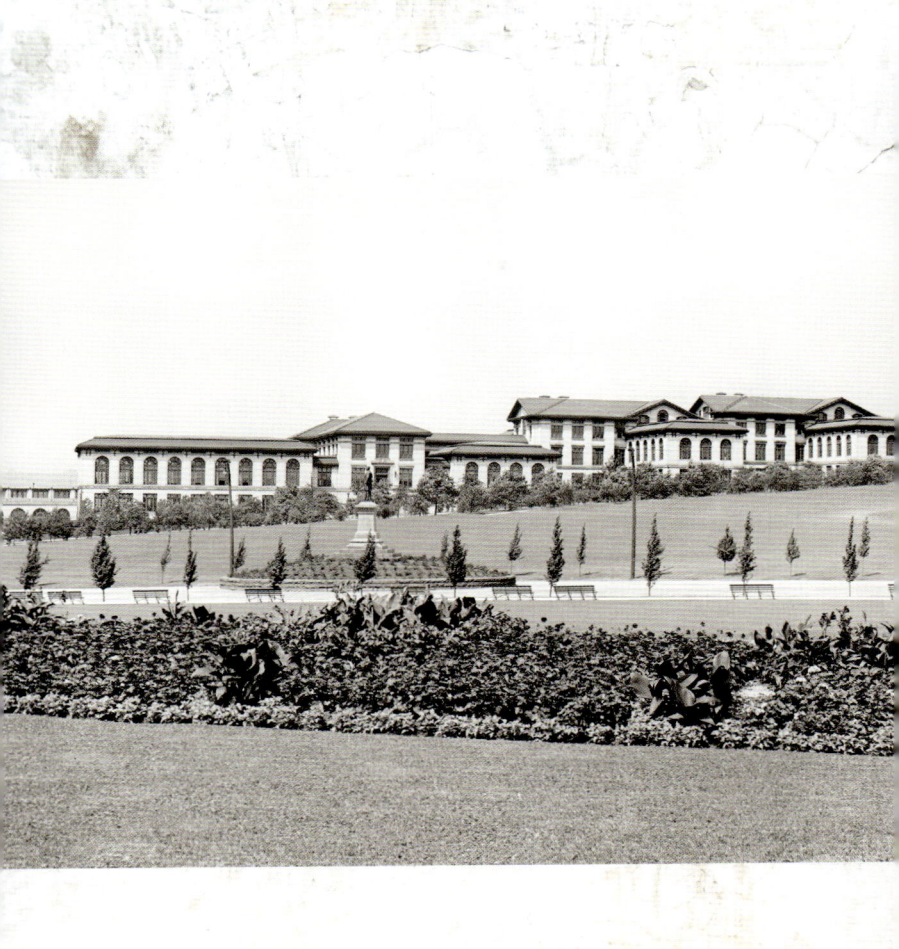

5

LOWER EAST SIDE

"There was absolutely nothing in Pittsburgh...for anybody with any kind of ambition." Philip Pearlstein

Andy couldn't get to New York quickly enough. One week after graduating from Carnegie Tech he was renting a cockroach-infested 'cold water' apartment in a tenement on the Lower East Side, together with his classmate, Phil Pearlstein. He arrived with a full portfolio of drawings, targeting fashion magazines. He struck lucky on his second day in the city. Tina Fredericks, art director of *Glamour* magazine, asked him to produce some drawings of shoes for the following morning at ten. She asked for revisions, also by ten the next day. Fredericks bought that set. Commissions began proliferating – art directors loved the fact that Andy got their world; there was no pretentious 'this isn't high art... am I prostituting myself?' about Andy. And he was quick – a workaholic – and the results brilliant. He also looked original and bohemian, in t-shirts and sneakers, à la Marlon Brando. If he got rejections, he would recover by simply going to church and praying for success. Andy was on a roll.

WHERE?
1950S LOWER EAST SIDE TENEMENT BUILDINGS,
MANHATTAN.

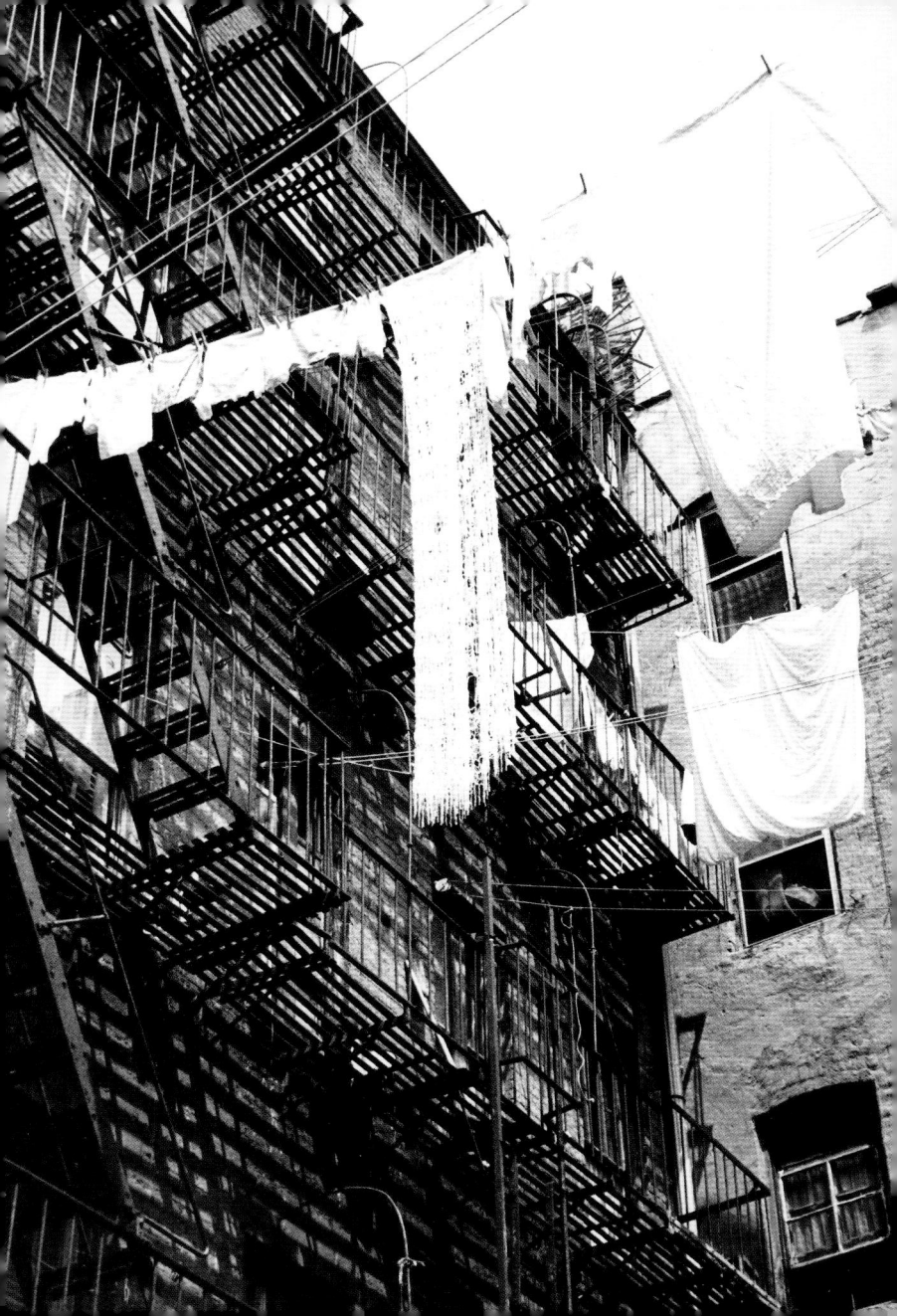

6

CHELSEA AND UPPER WEST SIDE

"[Andy's] career as fashion illustrator... made him realise the power of communication." **Vogue**

The *Glamour* article with Andy's shoes appeared at the end of August 1949, shortly after Andy turned 21. He and Pearlstein now moved to a room at the back of a loft being rented by a dance therapist at 343 West 21st Street, in then edgy and scruffy Chelsea. Andy was hustling a steady stream of commercial commissions during the day which he would then complete that evening. After a few short months in Chelsea he moved to a basement flat on the Upper West Side, at 74 103rd Street. Andy shared this with a bunch of dancers and somehow managed to squeeze a work table into the overcrowded space. After a few months he moved again, to East 24th Street, sharing with a classmate from Pittsburgh. Meanwhile work was going really well and in 1953 an illustration in the *New York Times* for a radio programme and album cover on drugs, entitled *The Nation's Nightmare*, won him a prestigious Art Directors Club gold medal. Andy's work was starting to get noticed and money started to flow.

WHERE?
THE UPPER WEST SIDE,
VIEWED FROM CENTRAL PARK,
MANHATTAN.

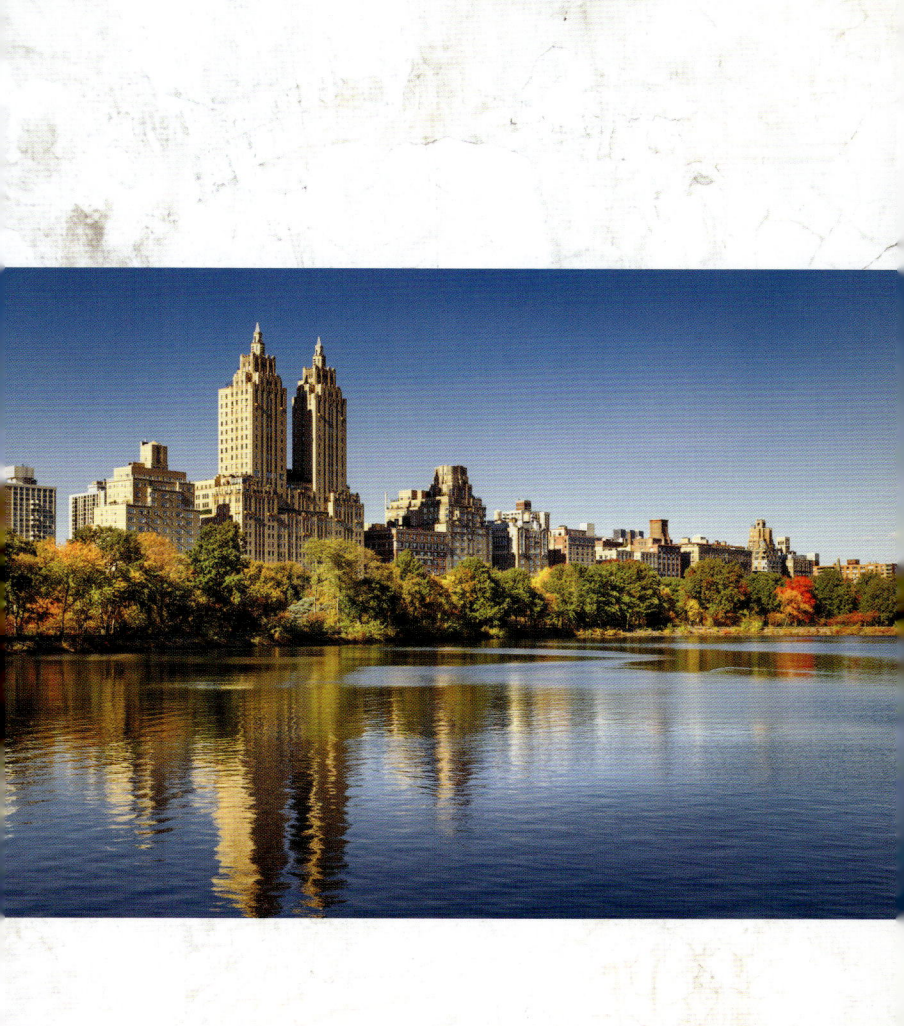

CAPOTE

"A hopeless born loser...the most friendless person I'd seen in my life."
Capote on Andy Warhol

Andy had always been obsessed with celebrities. He was an avid consumer of movie star magazines and, once in New York, he was intent on using whatever slender connections were to hand to try and meet some. Truman Capote, author of *Breakfast at Tiffany's*, was his special idol, and Andy began to send him daily fan letters offering to draw his portrait. He would then enclose drawings to accompany Capote's writings. He hung around the Capote apartment, trying to catch a glimpse of his idol, almost a premonition of the time that Jean-Michel Basquiat would do the same to Andy in the 1980s. Andy managed to get Capote's alcoholic mother to invite him up to their Park Avenue apartment one day, and met Truman when he returned home to find her drunk, discussing Andy's problems. Andy then began having daily phone calls with Truman until his mother, now finding the association with the low-rent Andy absurd, put a stop to it.

WHO?
TRUMAN CAPOTE,
PHOTOGRAPHED IN 1952

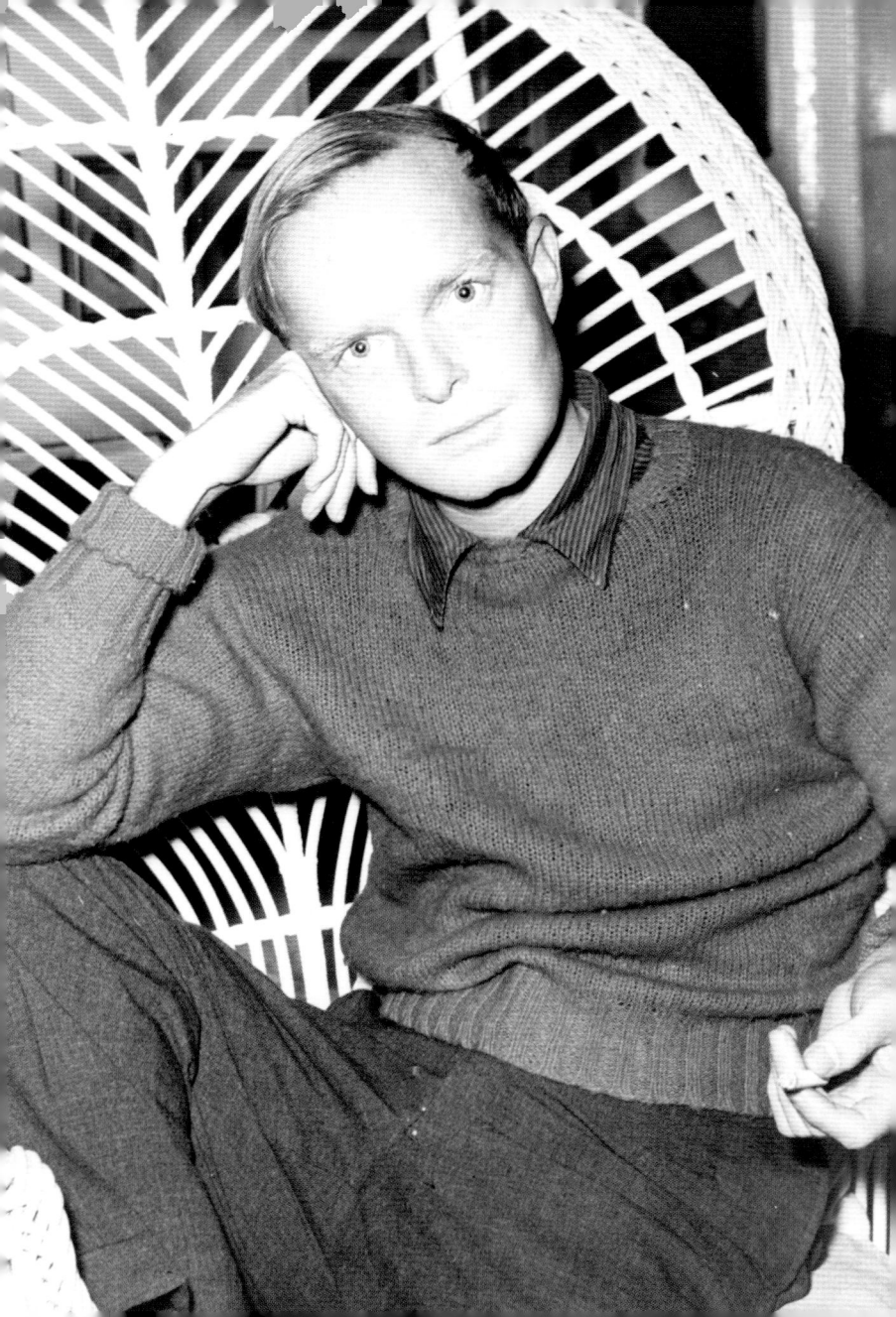

8

216 EAST 75TH STREET

"Homosexuality and other sex perverts [pose] security risks."
McCarthy Senate Subcommittee 1953

Andy had enjoyed the flat-sharing thing, but his sexuality was proving troublesome. It wasn't the fact he was gay – although homosexuality was illegal, there was a pretty open underground scene in New York in the early 1950s. It was more that he had trouble with physical intimacy. He was also intense, wanting to discuss emotional problems in depth, but found that his flatmates just wanted to fool around. A complete focus on his work was one way to cope. In 1952 Andy decided to move into his own apartment – another 'cold water' basement flat on Third Avenue and 75th Street. He solved the problem of potential loneliness by moving his mother, Julia, from Pittsburgh to live with him. Curiously, they shared a bedroom, each with their own mattress on the floor. But the arrangement worked. Julia ran the household, kept Andy entertained and encouraged him. Andy, conscious that the peasant-like Julia could prove an embarrassment, dealt with this by simply not inviting anyone back to the flat.

WHERE?
THE THIRD AVENUE ELEVATED RAILWAY, MANHATTAN.
(ANDY'S FLAT WAS A BASEMENT RIGHT NEXT TO THE TRACKS.
THE RAILWAY HAS SINCE BEEN DEMOLISHED.)

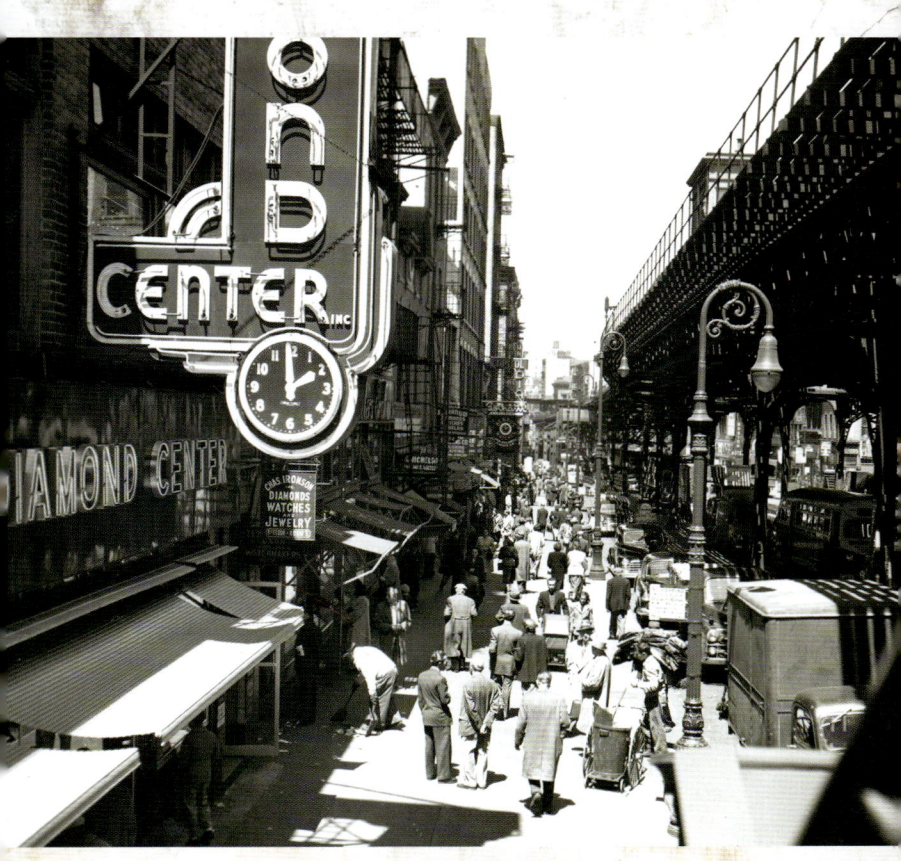

9

THE HUGO GALLERY

"The work has an air of precocity, of carefully studied perversity."
Art Digest

By the end of 1952 Andy was making over $125,000 (in today's terms) a year from his commercial art. It was time, he decided, to consider adding a fine art strand to his practice. With characteristic ease, he simply presented the clever director of the Hugo Gallery, Alexandre Iolas, with a portfolio of the drawings he had created for Capote. Iolas loved the work instantly, and agreed to shoo-in a show for Andy that June. Andy was in effect drawing no distinction between his commercial and 'fine art' styles; he didn't create anything new to go with what the gallery world or the critics might consider 'fine'. The opening of his show, on June 16th, didn't go as planned. Capote and his mother did not turn up (although they came later and admired what they saw). By most measures, Andy's first show was a flop: not a single piece sold. Andy was undaunted, however, and on the commercial side of things, Fritzie Miller, the influential artists' agent, now agreed to take him on. She would soon get his work into *Vogue* and *Harper's Bazaar*.

WHO?
THE CLEVER AND PERCEPTIVE ALEXANDRE IOLAS,
WHO GAVE ANDY HIS FIRST SHOW.

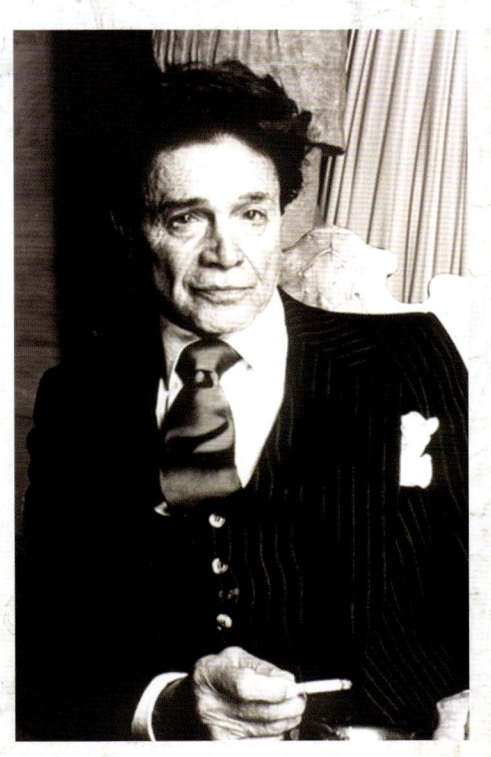

THE PLAZA HOTEL

"Nothing unimportant ever happened at The Plaza."
Anonymous New York quip

Partly as a result of Fritzie Miller, Andy's income rocketed to around $250,000 in today's terms. Andy now mixed the frugality of his childhood with some very deliberate excesses. He started taking breakfasts at The Plaza, eating at fashionable restaurants like Café Nicholson, and dressing in designer clothes (though cleverly he showed that they did not wear him by, for instance, distressing and paint-splattering expensive new shoes: Andy knew which signals to send out early on). He also rented a new, fourth floor and more spacious apartment, on Lexington and 34th Street. He filled the apartment with cats, which quickly multiplied; when a new one appeared Andy would try and hive it off to a friend. He and Julia still shared the bedroom and slept on mattresses on the floor. The main room served as Andy's chaotic studio, usually filled with ten or twenty cats, his art supplies and whatever gloves, handbags, scarves or shoes he had been commissioned to illustrate.

WHERE?
THE PLAZA HOTEL, WHERE ANDY WOULD
REGULARLY BREAKFAST AND BRUNCH.

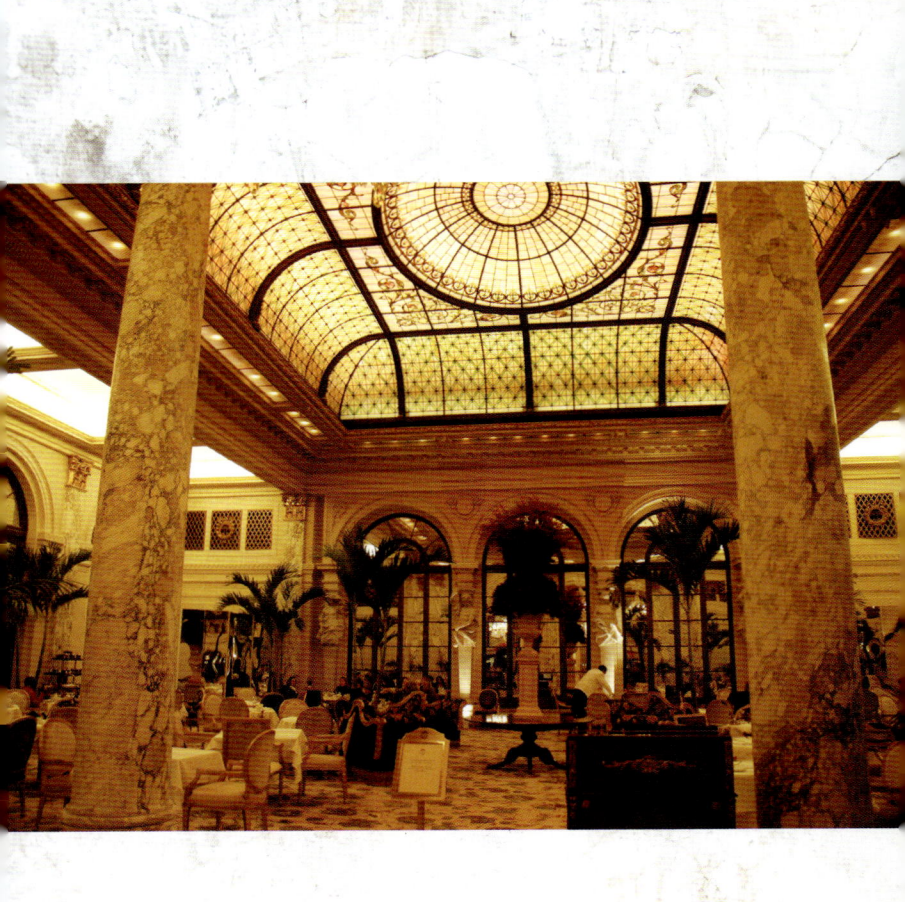

11

SERENDIPITY

"You never really knew who Andy was. His response was always, 'That's wonderful, that's fabulous,' but he didn't give much away." **Steve Bruce, owner.**

Andy's days now ran according to a regular pattern. He would rise at 9am, for a 10am appointment. Soon, knowing the habits of New York creative directors, he would know to casually turn up at 12.45pm. He usually grabbed lunch somewhere expensive, shopped for art supplies and then turned up for coffee and cakes at Serendipity, a café/shop/ice cream parlour on East 58th Street. In the evenings he would go to the theatre or ballet, or to parties. He would then work with total focus on returning home, going to sleep at 3 or 4am. Later, when working for I. Miller, one of the owners of Serendipity, Steve Bruce, invited Andy to frame any rejected shoe drawings, and to sell them in the shop. Many were bought by Serendipity regulars, the journalists and staffers from the nearby Condé Nast offices. Andy then developed a habit of knocking out new drawings on the café tables, to cover his Serendipity bills.

WHERE?
SERENDIPITY CAFE AND STORE,
EAST 58TH STREET,
MANHATTAN.

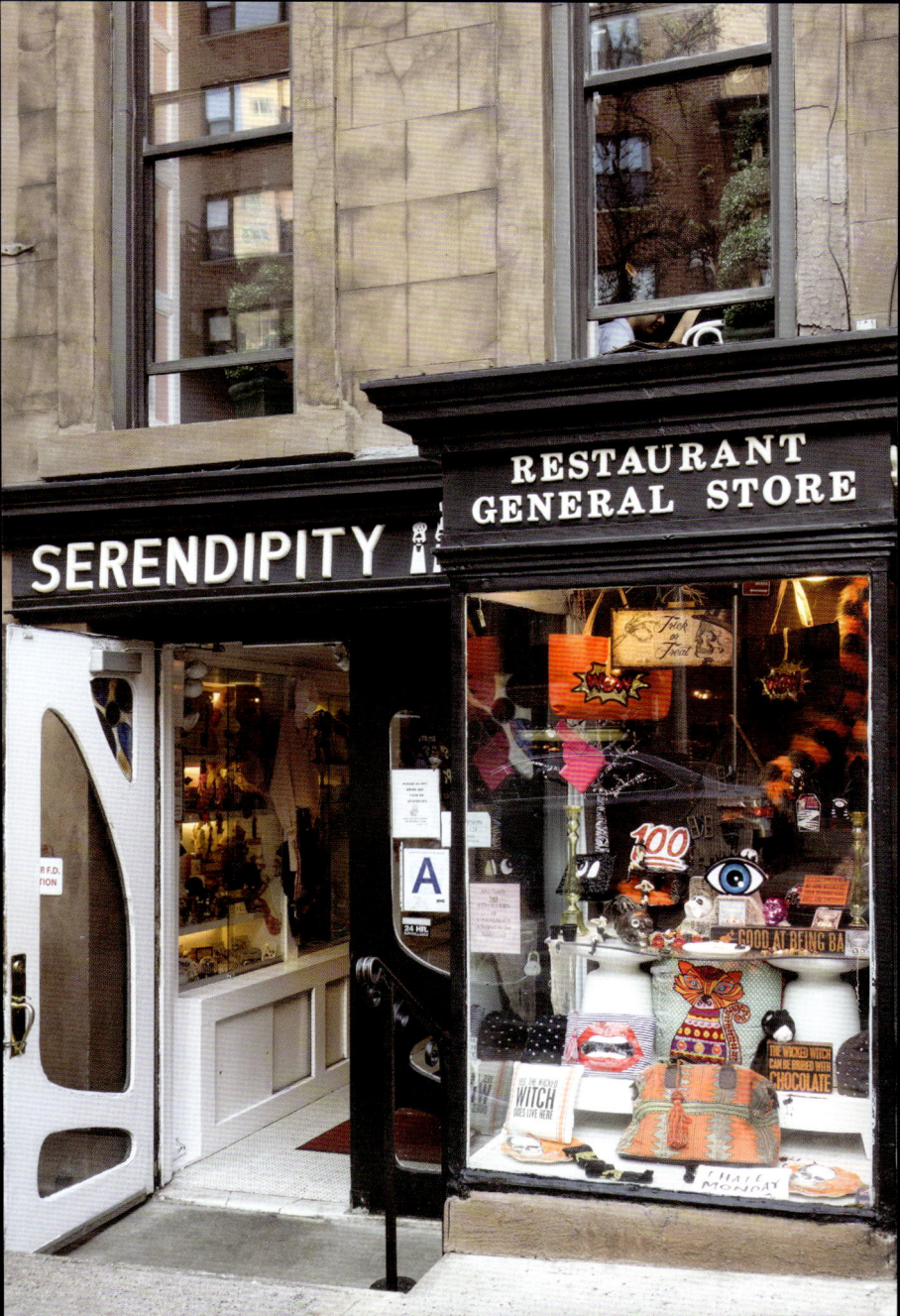

NEW YORK PUBLIC LIBRARY

"Andy sketched us screwing a couple of times." Robert Fleischer

In the absence of a sexual relationship, Andy found some satisfaction in voyeuristic drawing. He loved to ask friends if he could draw their penises or feet (he was somewhat of a foot fetishist). He loved to see and sketch erections. Meanwhile, for much of his commercial work, Andy would use the photo section of the New York Public Library. He would borrow photos and trace elements, returning them late so his plagiarism wasn't noticed. It was all about speed, pressaging his later production lines at The Factory. It was in the photo section that he met Carl Willers, assistant to one of the Library curators. They became friends, and then nervous lovers, Andy's first consummated relationship. It was hard with Julia floating around the apartment. Andy did manage a series of nude studies of Willers, part of Andy's overt exploration of gay themes in his work, a very provocative thing to do in 1950s USA. The sexual element of Andy's relationship with Willers petered out after a few months, but they remained friends.

WHERE?
MAIN READING ROOM,
NEW YORK PUBLIC LIBRARY,
MANHATTAN.

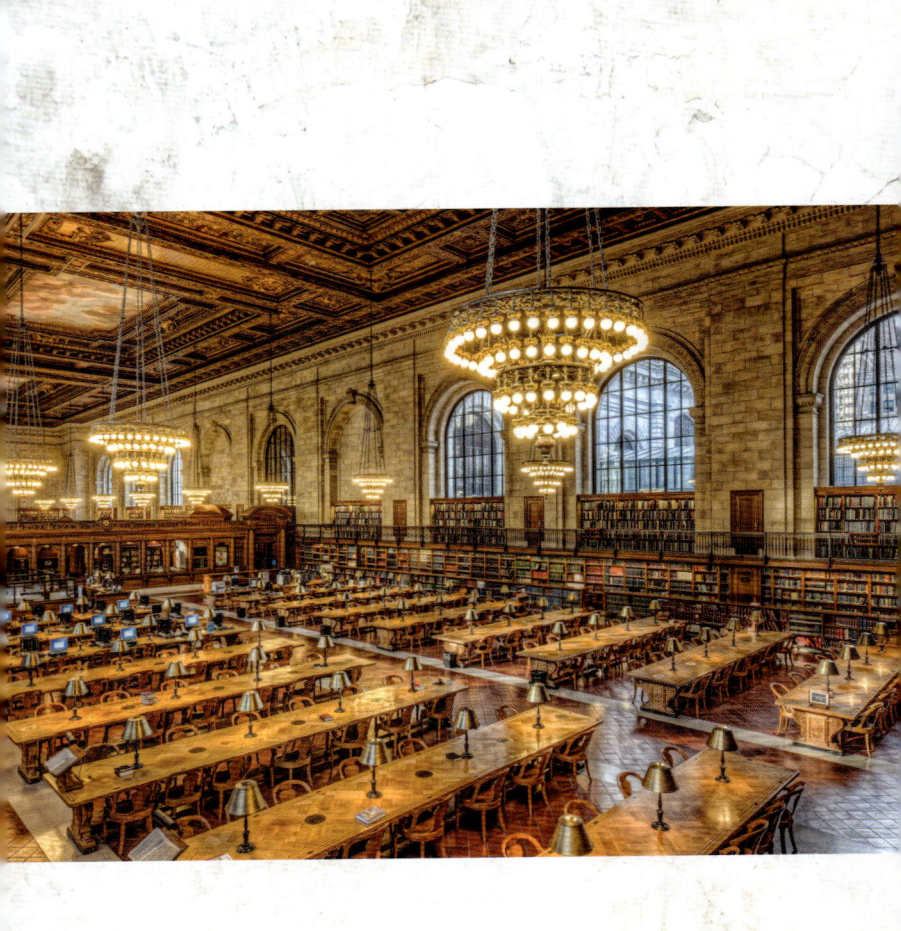

I. MILLER

"The effect was a sensational resuscitation of the I. Miller name."
Geraldine Stutz

I. Miller was a hugely successful designer shoe company, with 228 shops across the USA (including 16 in New York City), its HQ a palazzo on Broadway and 46th Street. In 1955 VP Geraldine Stutz and art director Peter Palazzo had decided the I. Miller brand needed a major reinvention, and they chose Andy to do this through a series of weekly illustrated advertisements in the Sunday *New York Times*. It was a huge account, worth $500,000 to Andy – in today's terms – per year. But it worked – I.Miller's public image was transformed. At the same time Andy was still pursuing a gallery career. His subject matter, often featuring homo-eroticism, made him hard to sell. He did receive the backing, however, of art dealer David Mann, who held a show featuring Andy's 'cocks with bows' drawings. They were surprisingly cheap – $60 a drawing – but only three sold. The contrast with the money from his commercial art could not have been more striking.

WHERE?
THE I . MILLER HEADQUARTERS BUILDING,
BROADWAY AND 46TH STREET,
MANHATTAN.

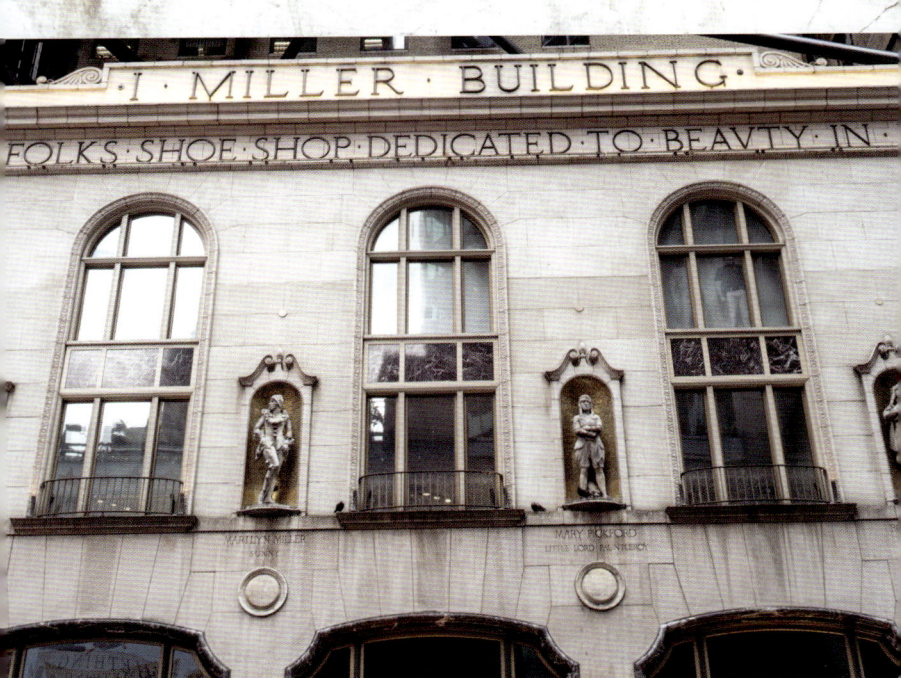

ANDY'S MANHATTAN 1949-1960

Manhattan was Andy's stomping ground. This is where he lived, became a hugely succesful fashion illustrator, and where he held his first solo show. Aside from his world tour with Charles Lisanby in 1956, Andy didn't really bother with travel. Everything he needed was immediately to hand, not least the advertising industry on Madison Avenue, which was on a rush of success at the vanguard of an explosion in US mass market, branded consumption.

KEY

- 🔴 Andy's New York galleries
- 🔵 Andy's apartments
- 🟠 Other Andy locations

ANDY'S NEW YORK GALLERIES

1 Hugo Gallery. E55th St. Andy held his first solo show here. Not a single work sold.

2 Loft Gallery. E45th St. Andy showed 3 times here in 1954.

3 Castelli Gallery. E77th St. Castelli represented top artists like Johns and Rauschenberg. He rejected Andy many times, but would later take him on.

4 Bodley Gallery. 1956-59. Andy held his Golden Slippers and Gold and Wild Raspberries shows here. All sold well.

ANDY'S APARTMENTS

1 Lower East Side. Andy's first New York flat, shared with Phil Pearlstein.

2 W21st St. Andy's second apartment, also with Pearlstein.

3 W103rd St. Andy shared this apartment with a group of dancers.

4 E24th St. Andy moved here with another Pittsburgh classmate.

5 E75th St. Andy lived here with his mother, Julia.

6 242 Lexington Avenue. Andy originally lived here on the 4th floor with Julia and then additionally rented the 2nd floor.

7 1342 Lexington Av. The first house that Andy bought, in 1959, for $600,000 in today's terms.

OTHER ANDY LOCATIONS

1 I. Miller Shoes HQ. Andy's contract with I. Miller, for advertising illustrations, was worth $500,000 a year.

2 New York Public Library. 5th Av. Where Andy did research and where he met his first boyfriend, Carl Willers.

3 Serendipity Cafe. E58th. A regular watering hole for Andy. Bruce the owner exhibited many of Andy's shoe drawings.

4 Plaza Hotel. Andy and Charles Lisanby regularly brunched here.

5 McBurney YMCA Gym. W14th St. Where Andy used to work out.

6 Barrow Street. Flat of Andy's photographer lover Ed Wallowitch.

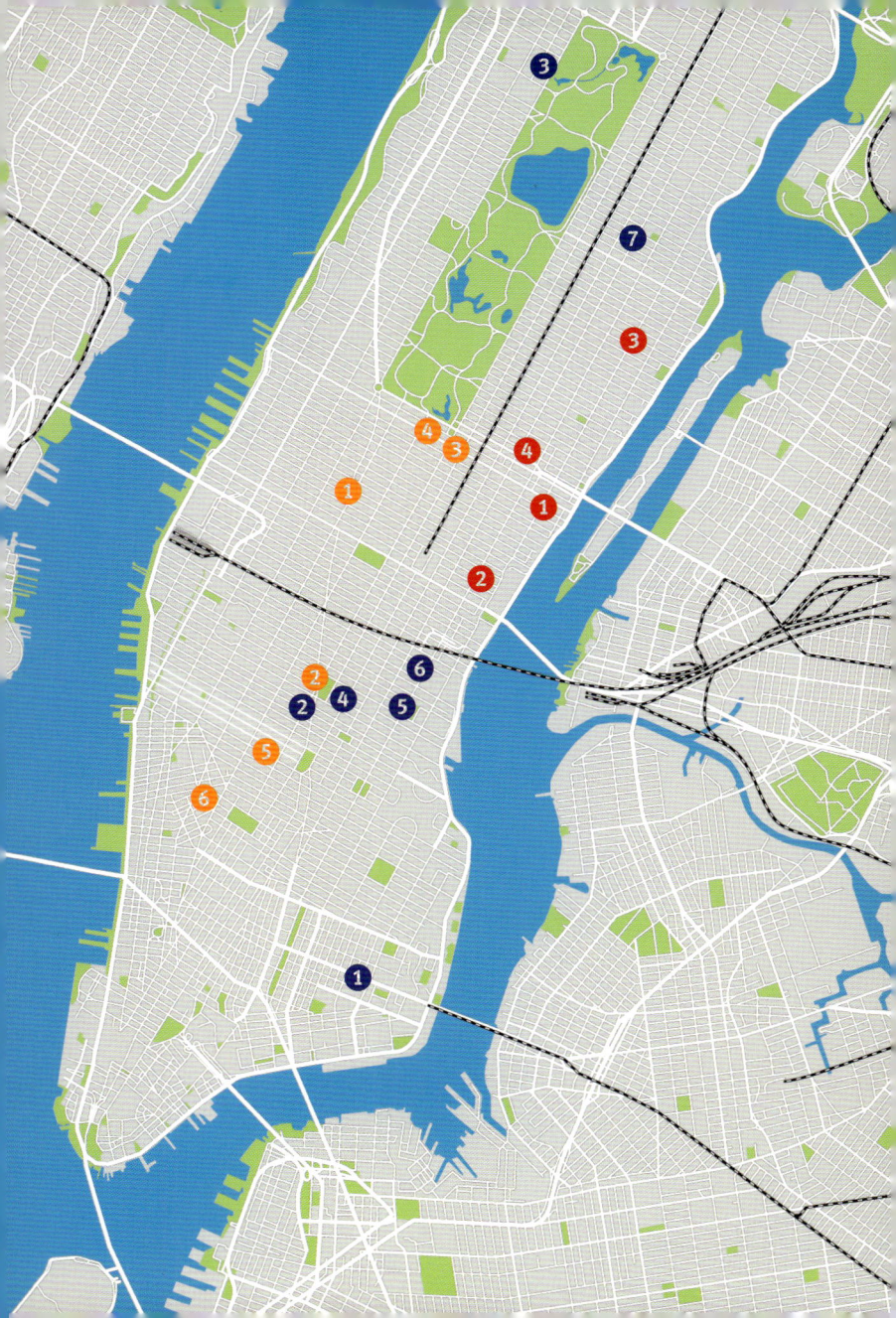

⑮

ANGKOR WAT

"Lisanby was also gay, but didn't have romantic feeling for Warhol."
L.A. Times

In 1956, as his relationship with Carl Willers faded, Andy fell madly in love with production designer and party animal, Charles Lisanby. They became instant friends, but Andy wanted it to go further. He and Charles decided on a round-the-world trip together, Andy hoping that an exotic location would relax Charles enough that he would succumb. They went to Bali, then to Cambodia and Angkor Wat, and then on to Calcutta. Charles became violently ill from food poisoning, and with it any idea that he and Andy would have sex evaporated. They escaped to Rome, via Cairo, where they ran into the early stages of the Suez crisis, nearly getting their passports confiscated. Charles spent two weeks recovering in Rome, with Andy in a grump. A trip to Florence was not a success. Amsterdam was a little more fun, but still no action for Andy. When they got home to JFK, Andy walked off the plane and out of customs, without even saying goodbye to Charles. This was a decisive gesture from Andy: from now on he wouldn't bother with love.

WHERE?
SUNSET AT ANGKOR WAT,
CAMBODIA.

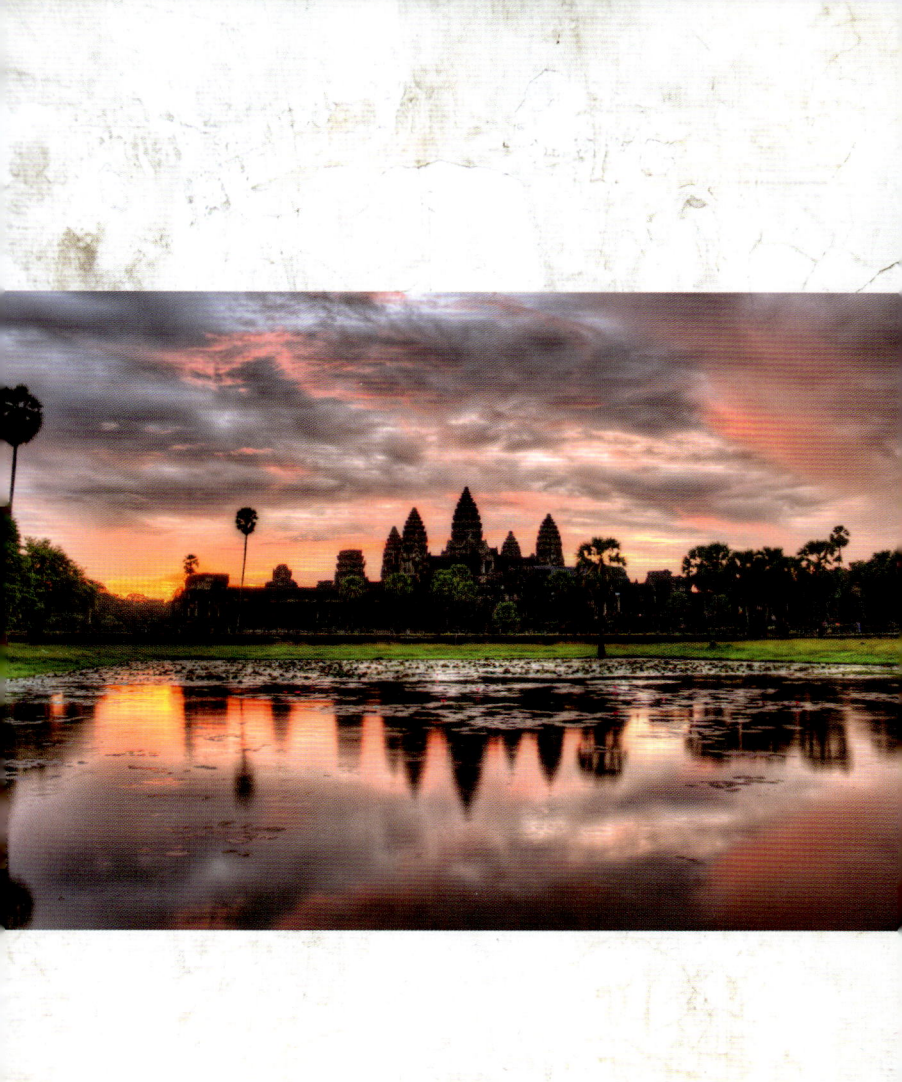

WORLD TOUR JUNE 1956

Andy didn't travel for travel's sake. Even on this world tour, his motivation was not the places they visited as much as the hope that Charles Lisanby would reciprocate Andy's deep feelings in sexy, exotic locations and consummate their relationship. Sadly, Lisanby didn't fall for Andy.

① NEW YORK
Andy and Charles flew west from Idlewild airport (now JFK).

② HONOLULU
From Honolulu Andy flew to Tokyo, where he changed planes for Bali.

⑥ CAIRO
The Suez military crisis was beginning as Andy and Lisanby travelled through. The pyramids held no interest for Andy.

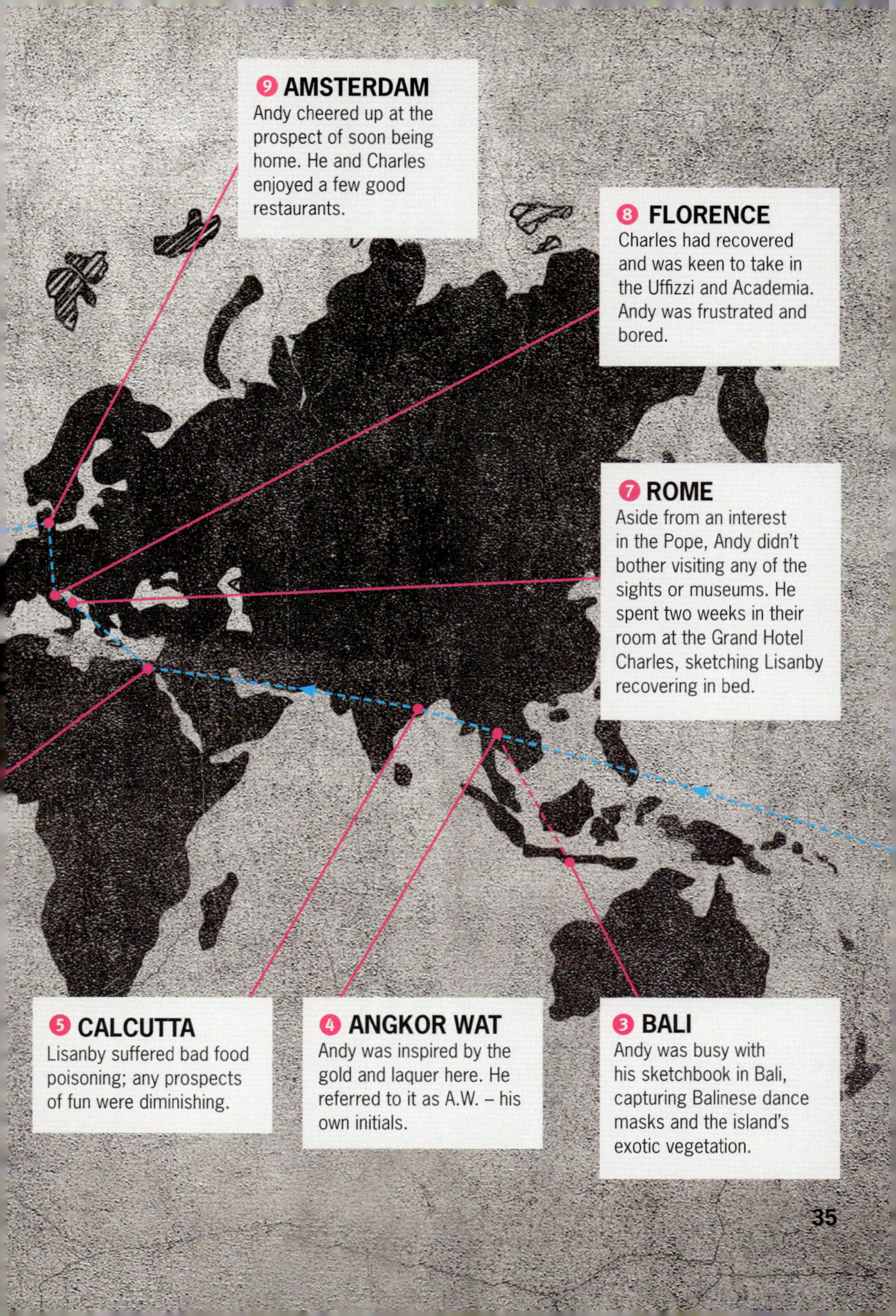

❾ AMSTERDAM

Andy cheered up at the prospect of soon being home. He and Charles enjoyed a few good restaurants.

❽ FLORENCE

Charles had recovered and was keen to take in the Uffizzi and Academia. Andy was frustrated and bored.

❼ ROME

Aside from an interest in the Pope, Andy didn't bother visiting any of the sights or museums. He spent two weeks in their room at the Grand Hotel Charles, sketching Lisanby recovering in bed.

❺ CALCUTTA

Lisanby suffered bad food poisoning; any prospects of fun were diminishing.

❹ ANGKOR WAT

Andy was inspired by the gold and laquer here. He referred to it as A.W. – his own initials.

❸ BALI

Andy was busy with his sketchbook in Bali, capturing Balinese dance masks and the island's exotic vegetation.

1956-1963

For Andy, the transition from commercial artist to 'fine' artist was not easy. Many of the overtly gay themes in Andy's art made him hard to sell (it's easy to forget that homosexuality was illegal in New York State in the 1950s and '60s; the Stonewall riots didn't happen until 1969 and same-sex sex was only decriminalised in 1980). But Andy was not easily deterred, even when his first solo shows weren't exactly a success: he just kept pushing. Then, in 1962, Andy had a breakthrough that would change the face of art for ever.

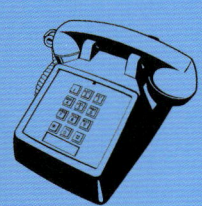

Andy and the Telephone

Andy was crazy about the telephone. It allowed him the mixture of detachment and intimacy which he craved. He went through a sequence of 'phone relationships,' notably with Truman Capote and, much later, with Paige Powell and Jean-Michel Basquiat. Most significantly for us, from 1976 he would call his diarist Pat Hackett every morning, recounting all the details of the previous day's (and night's) adventures, and including his taxi fares (just in case the tax authorities tried to question his expenditure).

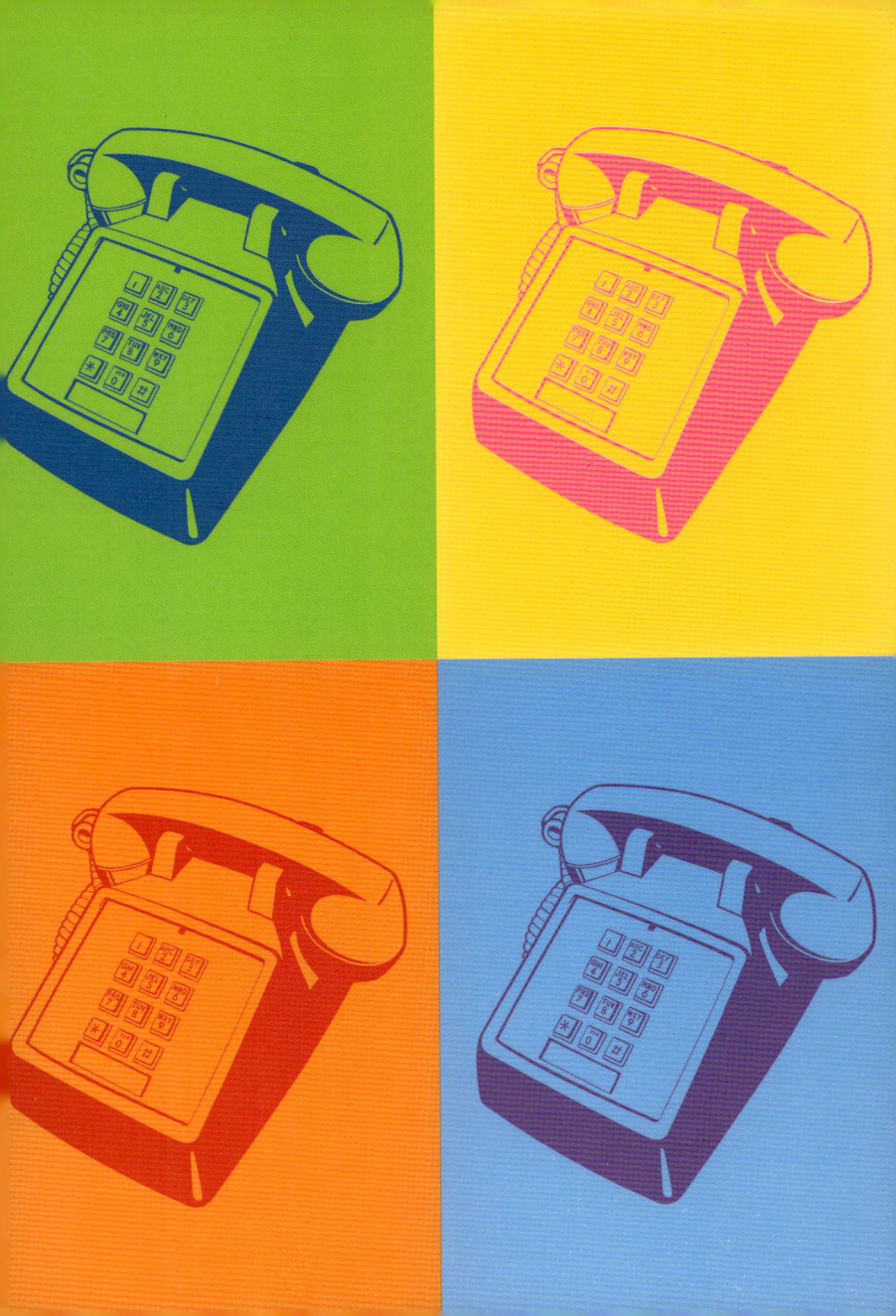

BODLEY GALLERY

"Oh God! They're not going to like these..."
David Mann quoting Andy

One thing to come out of the world trip was inspiration for Andy's next show at the Bodley Gallery, particularly the gold on black lacquer Andy had seen in Bangkok. Entitled the Crazy Golden Slippers Show (featuring shoes that echoed the characters of Elvis, James Dean, Mae West and Julie Andrews amongst others), it got Andy noticed by a wealthy potential clientele. The fact that he was toning down the gay emphasis in his work probably helped. The mega-wealthy makeup tycoon, Helena Rubinstein, commissioned a portrait, socialite D.D. Ryan bought a shoe drawing, and society fixer Jerome Zipkin commissioned one. Andy was featured in *Life* magazine, but, to his chagrin, was still described as just a commercial artist. It was proving hard to escape that straightjacket. Andy was now 27 and new younger artists, like Jasper Johns, were getting all the attention. Andy began to seriously worry that he wouldn't make it as more than a commercial artist.

WHO?
DAVID MANN, DIRECTOR OF THE BODLEY GALLERY, IN MANHATTAN, C. 1956.

38

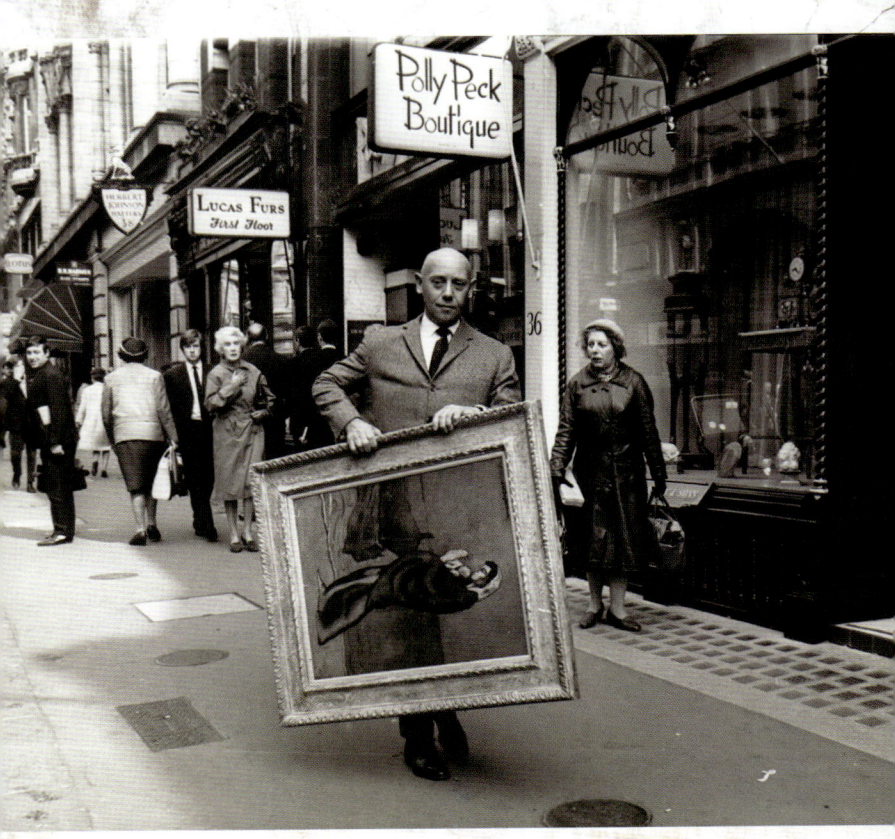

2

1342 LEXINGTON AVE

"I'm starting pop art...because I hate abstract expressionism. I hate it!"
Andy to Leonard Kessler

The I. Miller account gave Andy enough money to buy this townhouse on the Upper East Side, for $67,000. No sooner had he bought it than he lost the account – I. Miller had achieved their objectives, why keep very expensive Andy on their books? Even though Andy still had plenty of cash, the fickle competitiveness of the commercial world worried him and he began to get stressed about his bills. Now that he and Julia could live in comfort – he moved her into the basement – their relationship paradoxically soured. Andy was depressed again about the absence of love in his life. He began to see a shrink. More than anything, he began to feel excluded from the fine art world that seemed the answer, in so many ways, to his dilemmas. He was upset that the Johns/Rauschenberg abstract expressionist gang dropped him as a non-serious artist. It was from this swirl of emotions that a new Andy, Andy Warhol, the artist who would take New York by storm, was born.

WHERE?
1342 LEXINGTON AVENUE,
UPPER EAST SIDE,
MANHATTAN.

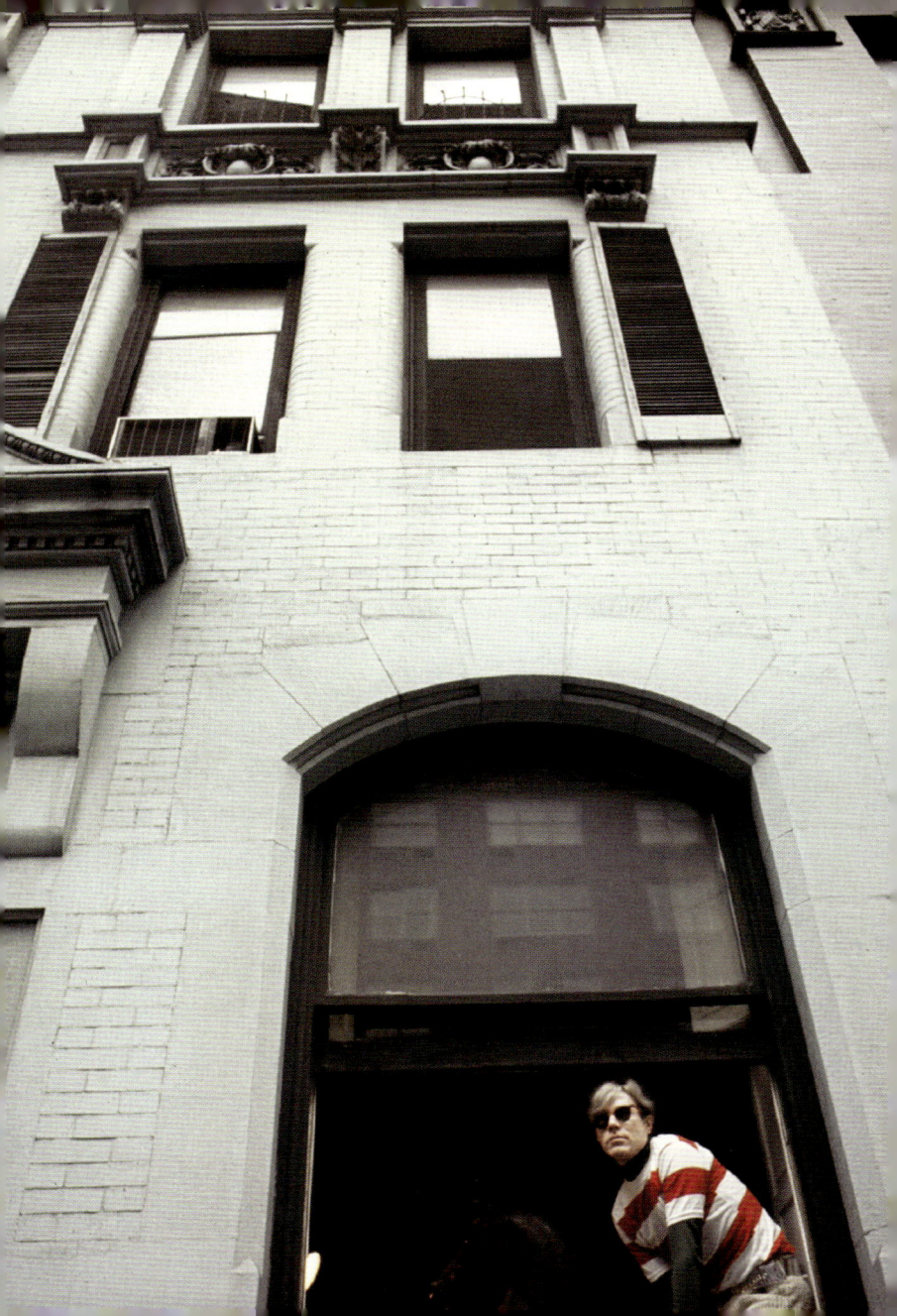

COKE

"...you know that the President drinks Coke, Liz Taylor drinks Coke, and just think, you can drink Coke too." **Andy Warhol**

Andy now underwent an image transformation. The first thing he did was have an operation to remove the bulbous end of his nose. Next the wigs were transformed – his signature askew silver hair replaced his attempts to look as though he had normal hair. He developed his stilted form of 'cool' speech – monosyllabic, full of pauses and "gee" and "wow." The interior of the Lex Avenue house was transformed – the windows of his living room/studio were boarded up to keep light out and Andy played rock LPs at full volume. Various new Andy works leant against the walls. These reflected a dramatic new direction – including two technically accurate 6-foot images of that iconic piece of US consumerism – the Coca-Cola bottle. Into this setting Andy invited Ivan Karp, the assistant to influential art dealer Leo Castelli. He loved what he saw. Castelli had just taken on an artist working with accurate depictions of cartoons – Roy Lichtenstein. Andy seemed to be working in a similar vein. The stirrings of a new direction for art were in the air.

WHAT?
AMERICAN MAGAZINE ADVERTISEMENT FOR COKE,
INSPIRED BY ANDY'S ICONIC WORK. ANDY AND THE COCA-COLA
COMPANY WOULD WORK TOGETHER IN THE '70S AND '80S.

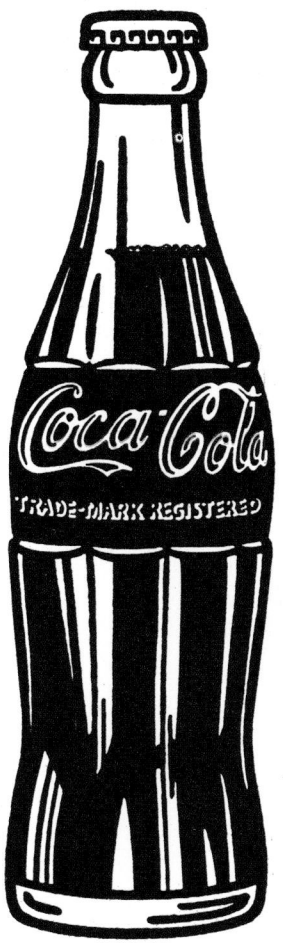

It's
the
real
thing.
Coke.

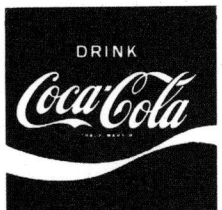

4

GELDZAHLER

"You will take me... I'll be back!"
Andy Warhol to Leo Castelli

Andy seemed to have a natural instinct for knowing how to work the system. One connection led to another. Karp brought various buyers to come and have a look at Andy's work. Most were dismissive. But Henry Geldzahler, assistant curator for 20th Century Art at The Metropolitan Museum, was not. He and Andy had an instant rapport when they met in July 1960. Henry was also gay, which may or may not have been a catalyst to their friendship, which became deep (although they were not lovers; this was a meeting of minds) very quickly. Andy and Henry talked on the phone every night before they went to sleep and every morning when they woke up. Henry, who was charged by the Met with being across new movements in art, thought Andy was a genius. All the New York galleries disagreed with him. Andy reached a low point when the powerful Leo Castelli, who had taken Lichtenstein on, decided to reject Andy. Even with powerful friends like Henry, Andy felt again that he was at risk of missing the future.

WHO?
HENRY GELDZAHLER,
ASSISTANT CURATOR OF ART AT THE MET, WAS AN
INFLUENTIAL FRIEND AND SUPPORTER OF ANDY'S.

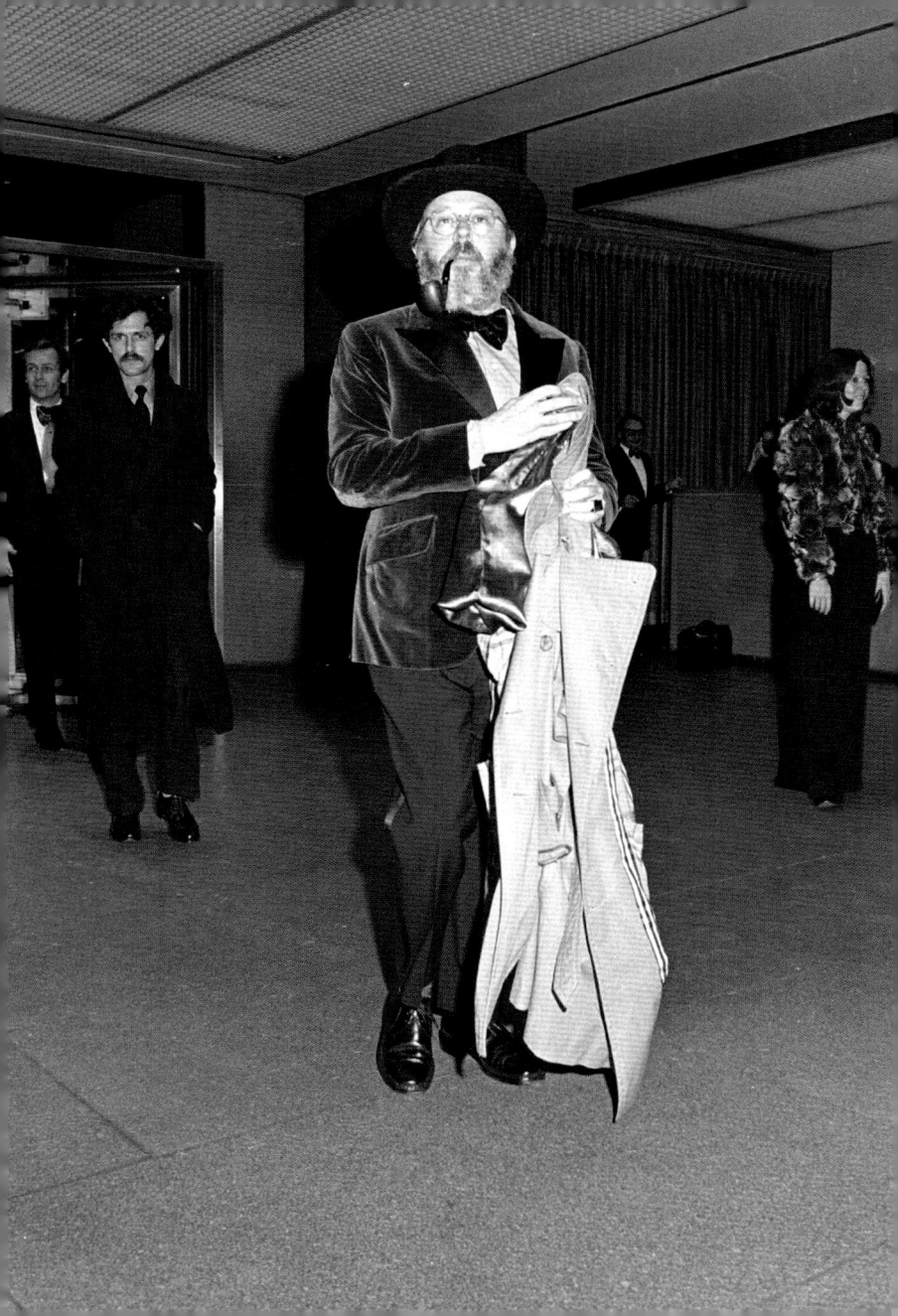

5

CAMPBELL'S SOUP

"You should paint something that everybody sees everyday... like a can of soup."
Muriel Latow

The idea for the soup cans did not come from Andy, but from Muriel Latow. Andy's genius was not to include soup cans in a bigger work, but to devote one canvas to each of the 32 varieties of Campbell's soup. The whole of the Lex Avenue drawing room was now devoted to his canvases. Art critics began to drop in and out. Dealers followed, notably Irving Blum who owned the Ferus Gallery in L.A.. Andy did not then have a dealer for his *Soup Cans*, so Blum offered him a show, pricing the paintings at $100 each. The paintings started to get wider publicity – being mentioned in a *Time* magazine article on pop art. The banality of soup cans began to create controversy – was this really art? Andy, with his highly tuned antennae for publicity, knew he was onto something, that he was achieving traction. That summer, Eleanor Ward from New York's Stable Gallery, dropped by the house, saw the work, and offered Andy the prized November slot for a show. This was potentially big. Fired up, Andy got to work.

WHO?
ANDY MODELLING WITH A CAMPBELL'S TOMATO SOUP CAN.

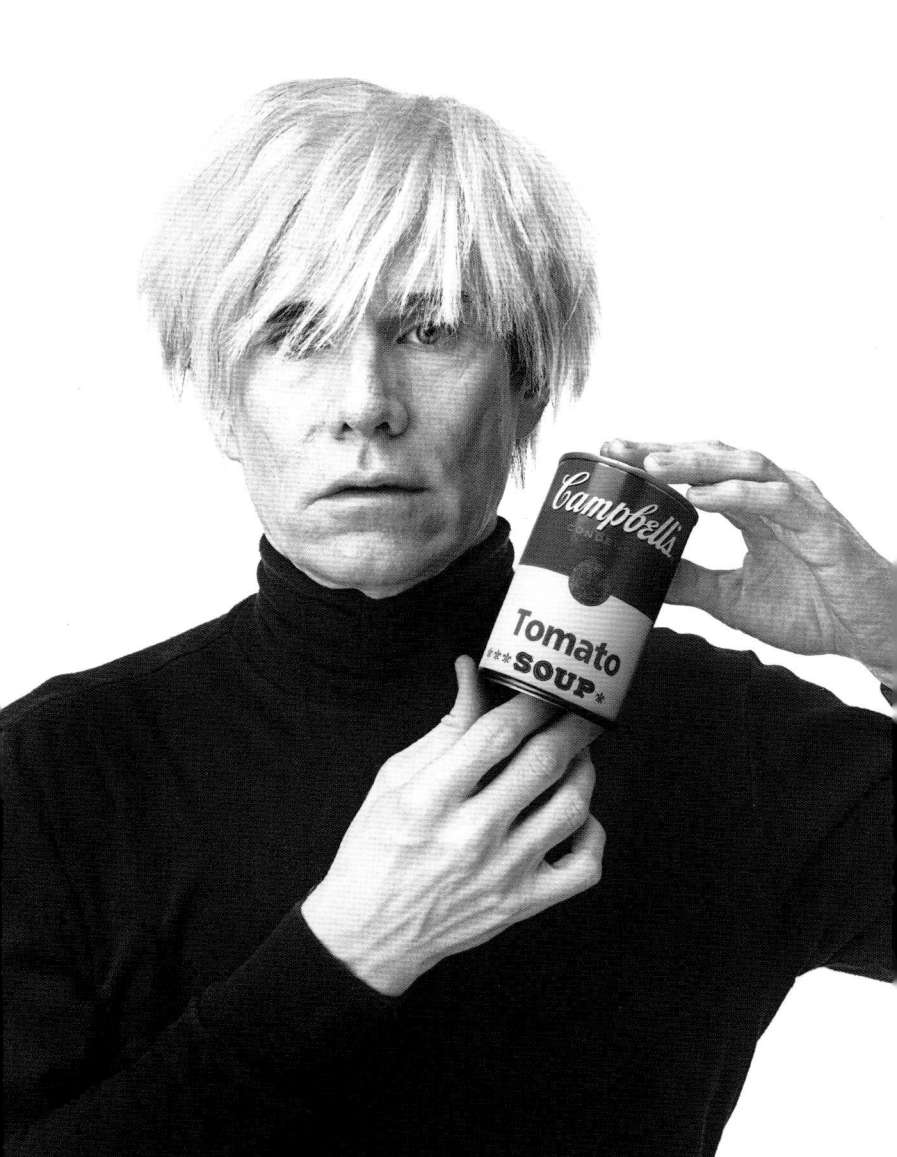

6

MARILYN

"Warhol's...silkscreens of Marilyn...[are] about as sentimental as Fords coming off the assembly line." Rob Sukenick

Andy was very productive that summer, in preparation for the show. He painted many seemingly banal subjects – Coke bottles, Green Stamps, more soup cans, 50 soup cans, 100 soup cans and dollar bills. The idea of repetition was taking root. His assistant, Nathan Gluck, then suggested silkscreening. Andy instantly got the advantages: many repeated images, but each one very subtly different; speed: art and painting as production line. When Marilyn Monroe tragically committed suicide on August 4th, 1962, Andy quickly knew what to do. He painted a series of repeated images of Marilyn – portraits of an icon, but, with repetition, commoditised. Marilyn as consumer product. He silkscreened her uniquely in gold in a small image, but also repeated 100 times on a 12-foot canvas. Next, he silkscreened the coke cans, soup cans, dollar bills and coffee cans, in all over 100 images, ready for the Stable Gallery show. When it opened in November, it was a huge hit. Nearly everything sold.

WHAT?
FRANK POWOLNY'S STUNNING IMAGE OF MARILYN,
USED BY WARHOL FOR HIS BRILLIANT MARILYN SCREENPRINTS.

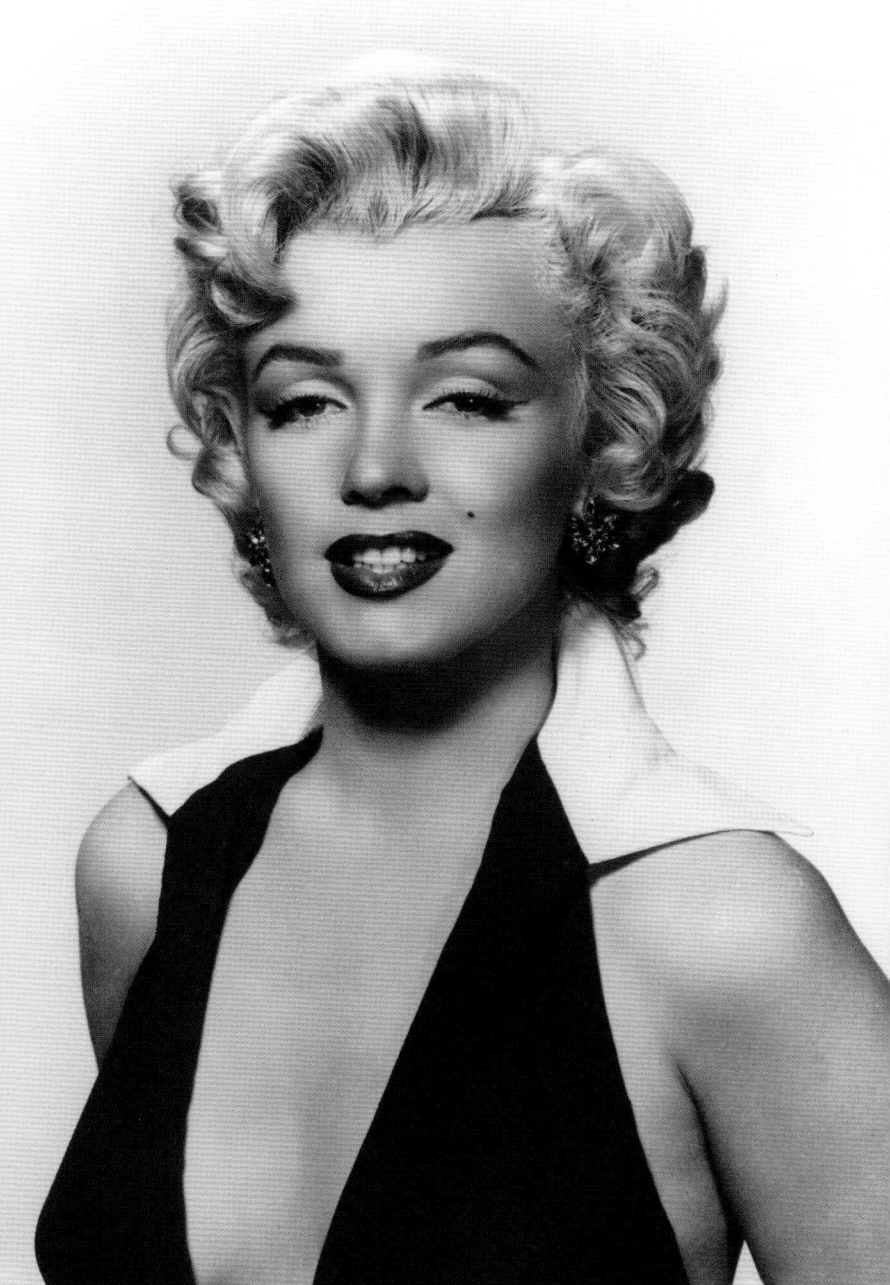

7

THE STABLE GALLERY

"One of the most talked about places to see art in New York."
The New York Times on the Stable Gallery.

From feeling that Lichtenstein and Claes Oldenburg had captured the pop art zeitgeist before him, Andy now eclipsed them with the Stable Gallery show. The press were outraged and Andy Warhol was portrayed as the fraudster-in-chief. This wasn't art, they screamed. Most pleasingly for Andy, the abstract expressionists who had snobbishly given him the cold shoulder, now seemed like yesterday's news. Their supporters derided his work as 'a vacuous fraud.' The Campbell's soup cans were the main targets for their attacks. Other artists hated Andy – they had worked hard, trying to create 'real' art, and now the ground had been cut from beneath them. Andy also made a wonderful target, with his deliberately stilting, content-free interviews and his other-wordly silver wig look. But Andy knew there was really no such thing as bad publicity. As the columns attacking Andy multiplied, so did his status. The party invitations to the cream of New York society flowed in. Andy was in his element: for him parties were work.

WHO?
ANDY, C. 1962.

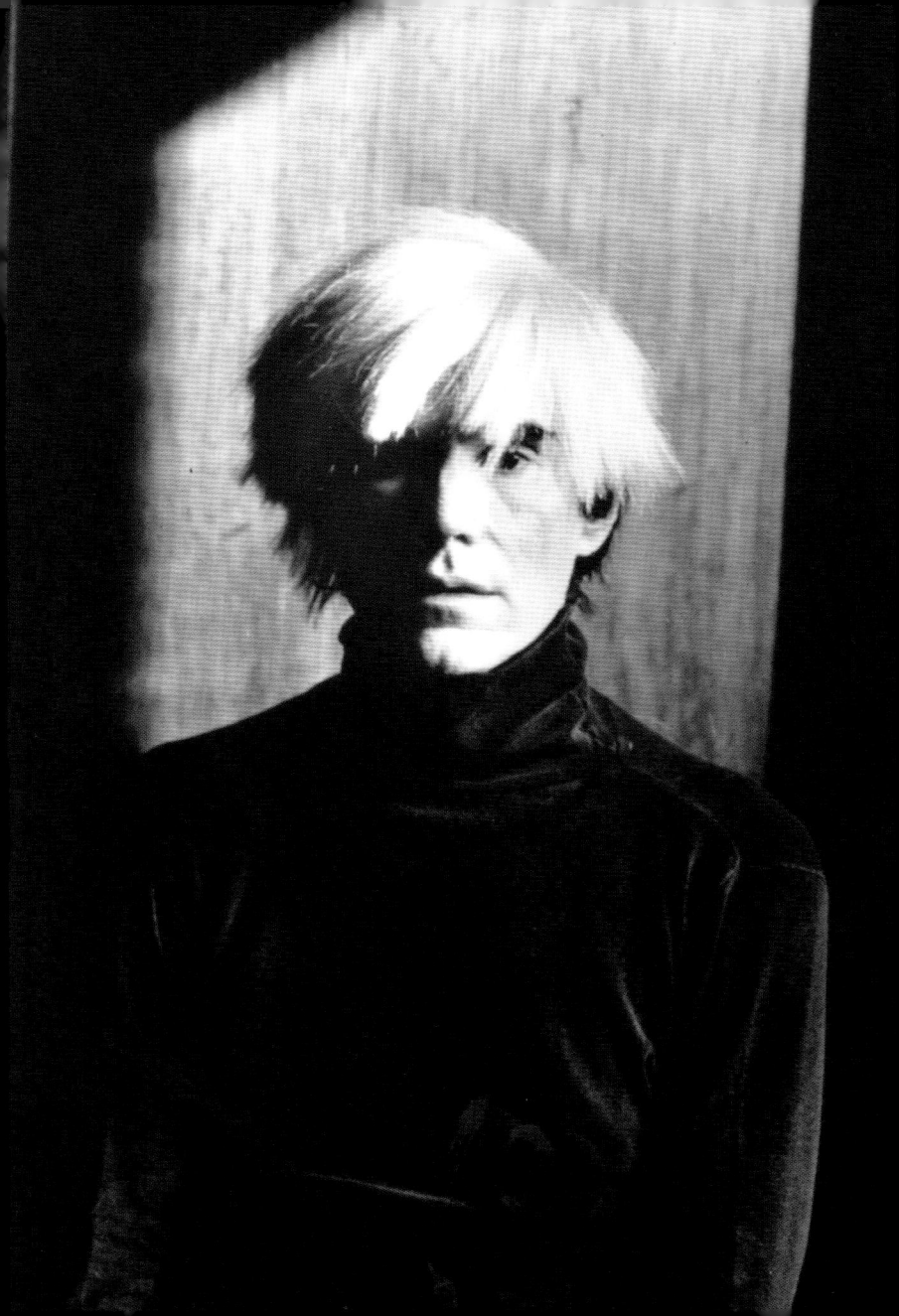

8

THE FIREHOUSE

"Everytime you turned on the radio they said... 4 million are going to die."
Andy Warhol

With his increased rate of production, it was clear to Andy that working at home was no longer an option. He rented a space in this disused firehouse on 87th Street, a few minutes walk from the house. It was really uncomfortable – no heating – and the roof leaked. But the space was big. Andy hired a new assistant, Gerard Malanga, who had silkscreen experience. Andy produced some seminal works here – his 6-foot high pictures of Elvis as cowboy with a drawn revolver, repetitive reproductions of the Mona Lisa, portraits of Ethel Scull (the Sculls became avid early collectors of Andy's work) and Robert Rauschenberg. Andy also experimented with pornography – he went to see movies being shot, so he could get the raw aesthetic. He then turned to the other side of US life: sensationalised death and disaster in the press. Suicides, car crashes, electric chairs, even tuna-can poisonings, all received the Andy treatment. Each silkscreen took about four minutes. But the Stable Gallery refused to show them: too grim to hang on a living-room wall. They would in time become his most prized works.

WHERE?
HOOK AND LADDER FIREHOUSE BUILDING,
87TH STREET AND LEXINGTON AVENUE, MANHATTAN.

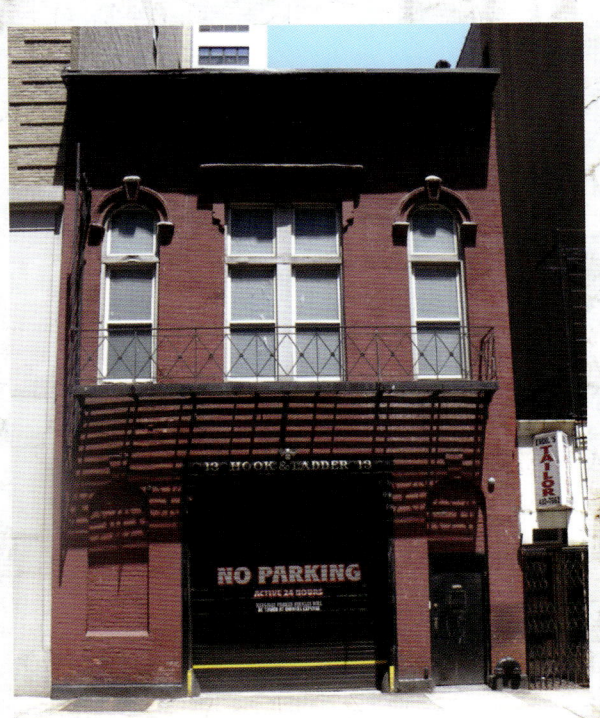

ROUTE 66

"Too many big shots die in planes."
Julia Warhola

Pop art was now being noticed in California and Irving Blum decided to capitalise by giving Andy a second show at the Ferus Gallery. A star-studded launch was planned, including Dennis Hopper. Andy, obsessed with Hollywood, couldn't resist going. The problem was that he now developed a fear of flying. Driving, à la Kerouac *On the Road*, was the answer. Andy picked two of his druggier friends to do the driving, Taylor Mead and Wynn Chamberlain. Gerard Malanga also joined them. They stayed in motels and ate in diners. The car was a scruffy Ford station wagon, with a mattress in the back; the route: St Louis–Kansas-Oklahoma–Texas–New Mexico–Arizona–Los Angeles. Andy was the only one not stoned and he showed no interest in visiting anywhere, often just sitting in his motel room, staring. He saw the experience as 3,000 miles of silent road trip movie. They took 4 days, with one near-fatal near-miss, before they arrived in L.A. and checked into the Beverly Hills Hotel. The show was a failure – why is not clear – but not a single work sold. Movie stars, decided Andy, were really rather stupid. They drove back, another 3,000 miles. But this gave Andy time to think. He needed more space, not just to paint, but to make movies.

WHERE?
ROUTE 66. NEVADA DESERT.

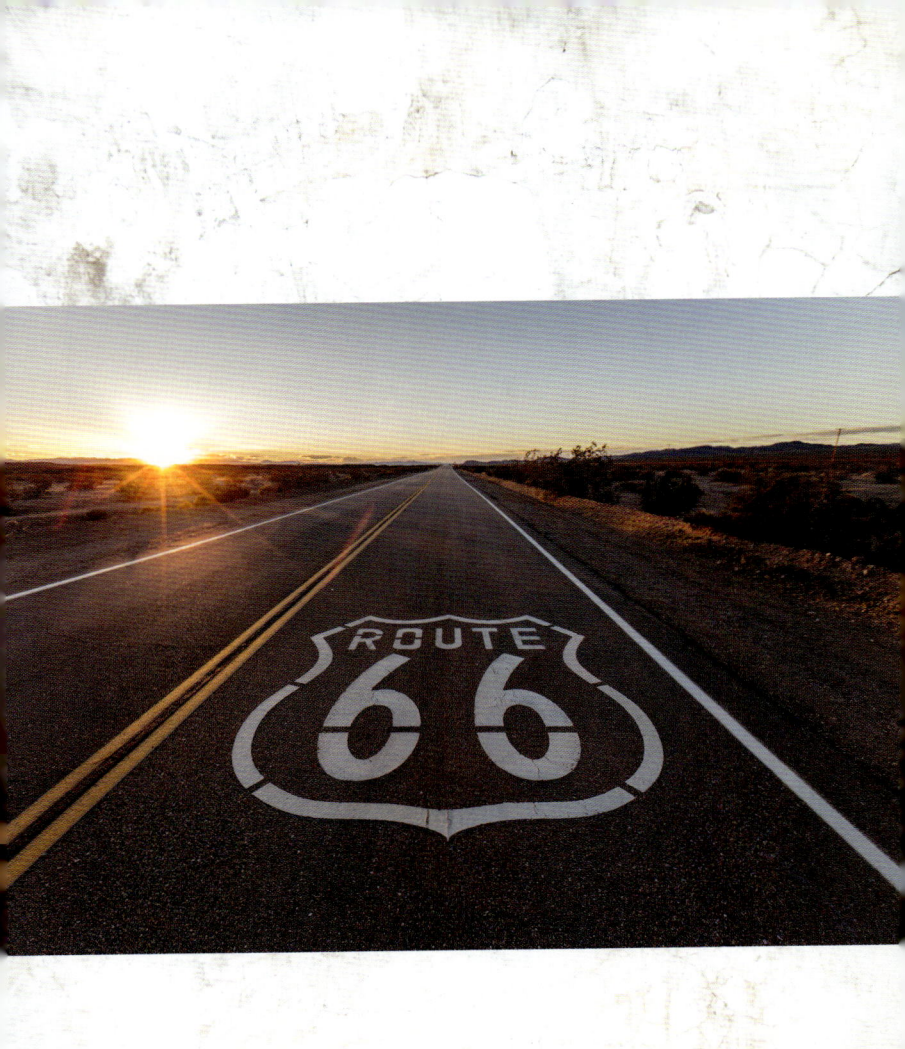

1963-1969

The trip to Hollywood had given Andy the idea for the Factory. Andy now became a voracious avant-garde movie maker – he would go on to make hundreds, using his 16mm Bolex camera. Most were never released. The ones that were – including *Sleep*, *Blow Job*, *Empire*, *Poor Little Rich Girls*, *The Chelsea Hotel*, *Lonesome Cowboys* and *Blue Movie (Fuck)* – redefined what a movie could be. Many were shot in real time, sometimes on split screen, usually improvised, showing scenes of shooting-up, sex, banal conversation, or just watching one of his 'stars' getting up in the morning. The Factory became a party scene, a magnet for misfits, wannabes and drag queens, many on crystal meth, cocaine and heroin. Andy didn't partake, although from 1963 he did take a daily dose of Obetrol, a then–legal amphetamine diet pill. He treated this cast of characters, some of whom he annointed as 'Superstars,' as the subjects on whom he would train his lens, his take on the brittle, destructive nature of fame and celebrity. Many got even more screwed up in the process. One, Valerie Solanas, shot Andy at the Factory in 1968. He was very lucky to survive.

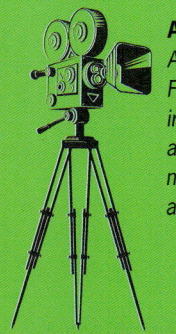

Andy and the Movies
Andy loved movies. He would go and watch art house films at the Film-makers' Co-op, and reflected that he could do so much better, by ironically sending up the whole art house genre, whilst pushing at the acceptable depiction of drugs, sex, taste and violence. He bought his first movie camera, a 16mm Bolex, in June 1963, and started making movies a month later.

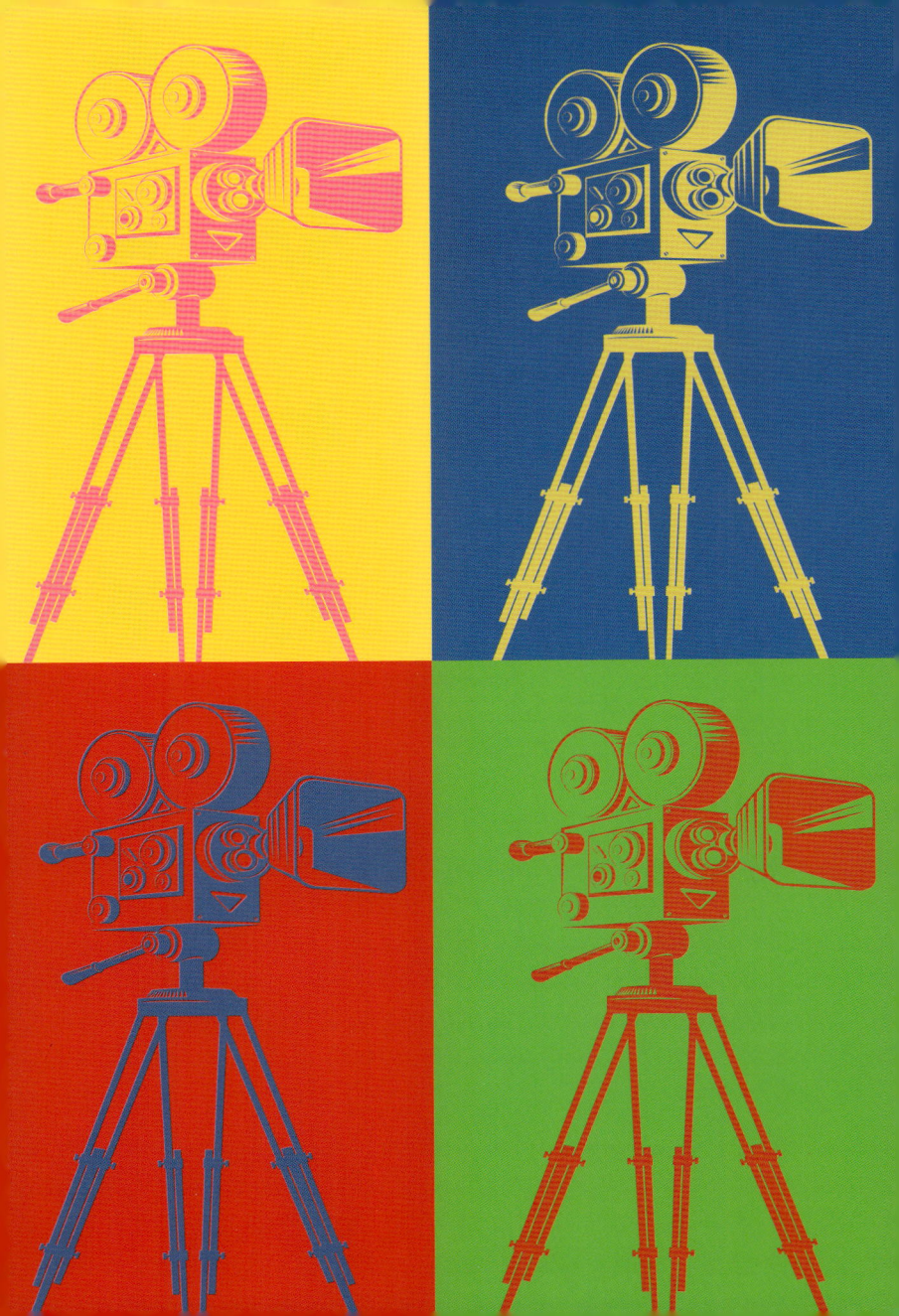

1

THE FACTORY (NO. 1)

"When he went into making films...he became a whole different person."
Carl Willers on Andy

Andy's new space, formerly a hat factory which he, naturally, named the Factory, was on the fifth floor, at 231 East 47th Street. It was big, 100ft by 40ft, and marked a new departure for Andy. The walls were all silver, covered in foil. Opera or rock blasted out non-stop. Andy changed his look – S&M leather jacket, skin-tight black jeans, T-shirts, high-heeled boots and that wig, more silver than ever. Before he'd gone to L.A., he had created a six hour film on his Bolex 16mm camera, of John Giorno sleeping, entitled *Sleep*. Once at the Factory, he followed this with *Blow Job*, a camera trained on Giorno's face as he was blown. *Hand Job* followed *Blow Job*. Word got out that there was a new underground film maker in New York. One innovation was shooting at 24 frames per second, but playing back at 16. The effect was haunting. The parties for the launches of his movies turned into a scene. If you needed to identify the avant garde in NYC, it was here. The Factory had captured the zeitgeist and Andy was the inscrutable maestro in the midst of it.

WHERE?
ANDY WITH THE CAST OF *CHELSEA GIRLS* AT THE FIRST FACTORY, EAST 47TH STREET, MANHATTAN.

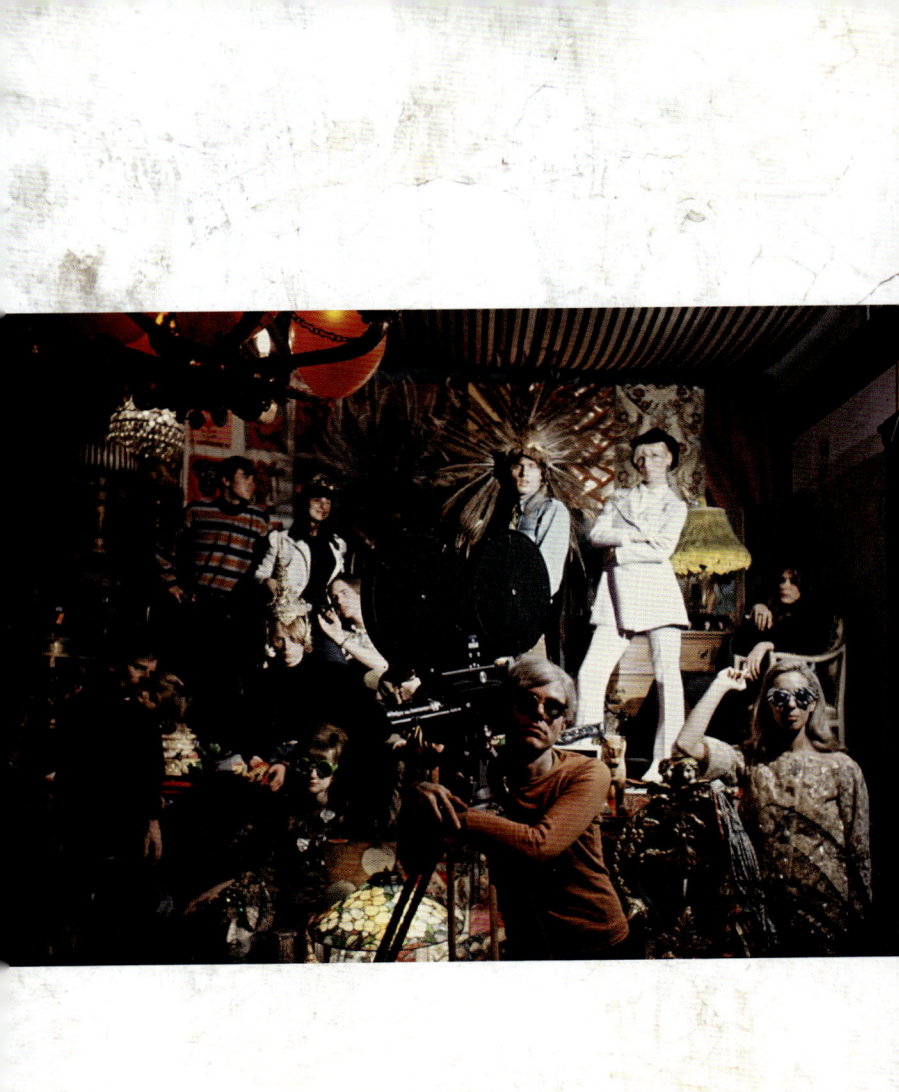

2

THE ASSEMBLY LINE

"He had a genius of...making a work of art of the whole climate here in New York."
Leo Castelli

The Factory started to fill with a cast of characters, all somewhat damaged, mostly on speed or crystal meth, who wanted to be in Andy's movies, or rich kids who just wanted to be around Andy. These included the 'acrobatic verbalist' and actor, Ondine; Brigid 'Polk' Berlin (her dad ran the Hearst Corporation); model and friend of the Rolling Stones 'Baby' Jane Holzer, and Billy 'Name' Linich, who Andy appointed as the Factory's manager. Andy would take the better looking 'members' to parties, ensuring good press. He also started asking visitors to the Factory to drop their pants, so he could photograph their cocks. His old friends felt dismayed at this new persona. They started to fall away. But the Factory also lived up to its name. Andy began organising it as an assembly line for art. His new venture was sculptures – of packaging – silkscreened, with plywood frames, but as identical to the originals as possible. 400 were created, most famously of Brillo pads, for his next show at the Stable Gallery.

WHERE?
ANDY AT THE FACTORY IN 1964, MANHATTAN.

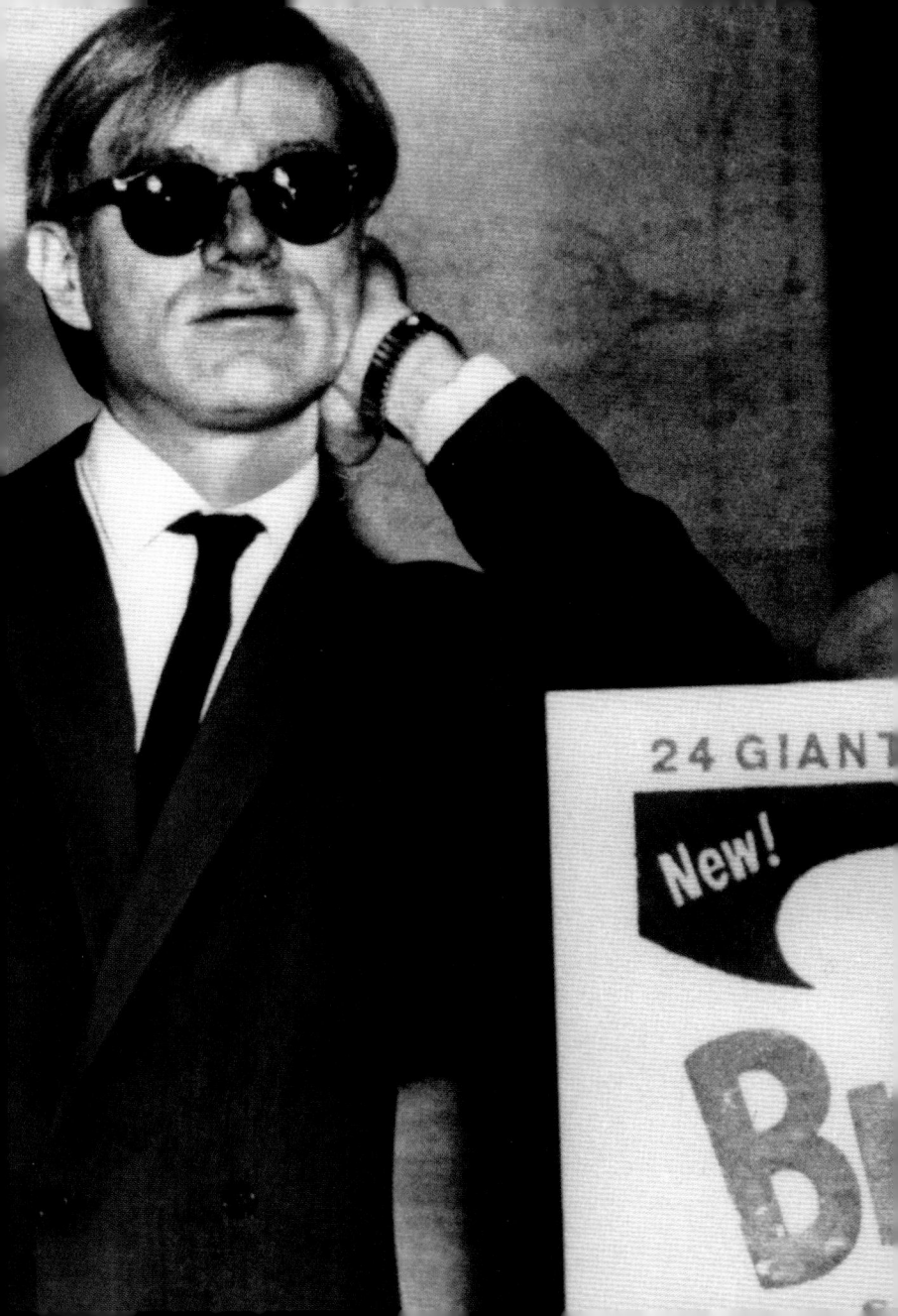

3

EMPIRE

"The Empire State Building is a star.
It's an eight-hour hard-on."
Andy Warhol

The Brillo boxes were considered an artistic success, but they didn't sell. Andy decided he needed a new dealer, and switched, showing total ingratitude, from Eleanor Ward of the Stable, to Leo Castelli. Castelli got what Andy was doing, turning his persona and the Factory into as much a work of art as the art itself. Andy became a manipulative svengali at the heart of the Factory, which in effect now became a movie studio. The movies became more outrageous. *Couch*, featured people fucking on the Factory couch, including then taboo hetero anal sex and, more provocatively for the time, sex between men. Whilst the camera rolled, Andy would just sit and watch. Andy started manipulating his 'stars,' one minute having them in his movies, the next dropping them in favour of someone else. He recognised that they all wanted to be used. And whilst they 'worked' for Andy, he never paid them. In the midst of what was in essence a crazed cult, Andy shot the amazingly calming *Empire* – the Empire State Building shot in real time, from dawn to dusk.

WHERE?
THE EMPIRE STATE BUILDING, 5TH AVENUE,
MANHATTAN.

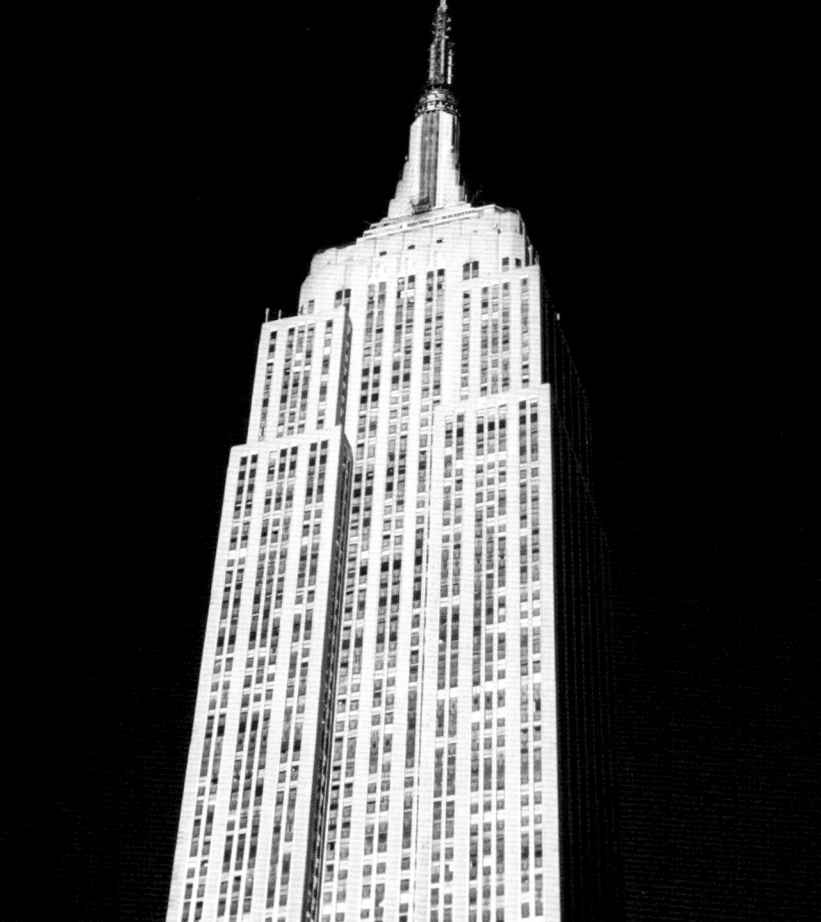

4

LEO CASTELLI GALLERY

"The flower paintings are...beautiful. The artist is a mechanical Renaissance man, a genius." **The Village Voice**

Unlike his last show at Stable Gallery, Andy's first show at Leo Castelli was a sell-out. Maybe this was because his subject was flowers, based on photos of poppies by Patricia Caulfield. He also received the sixth Annual Film Culture Award, for his contribution to cinema. This completely outraged many members of the renowned Film-Makers' Co-op. Andy now added *Screen Test* and *Harlot* to his film repertoire, both featuring drag queen Mario Montez. Andy was cynically unfazed by the death on LSD of Factory regular Freddie Herko – "Why didn't he tell me? We could have...filmed it!" When Andy met a – according to Ronnie Tavel – "high-class faggot" who had tried to commit suicide, Andy conceived *Suicide*, a movie where the man talked on camera, whilst the events and people who had prompted him to slash his wrists 23 times were re-enacted. It was hardly surprising that many thought 'Drella' (Dracula/Cinderella), as he was now nicknamed, was essentially ice-cold and evil, not caring who was screwed or used in the name of his 'art'.

WHO?
THE CLEVER, URBANE LEO CASTELLI,
UNDISPUTED MAESTRO AMONGST NEW YORK ART DEALERS.

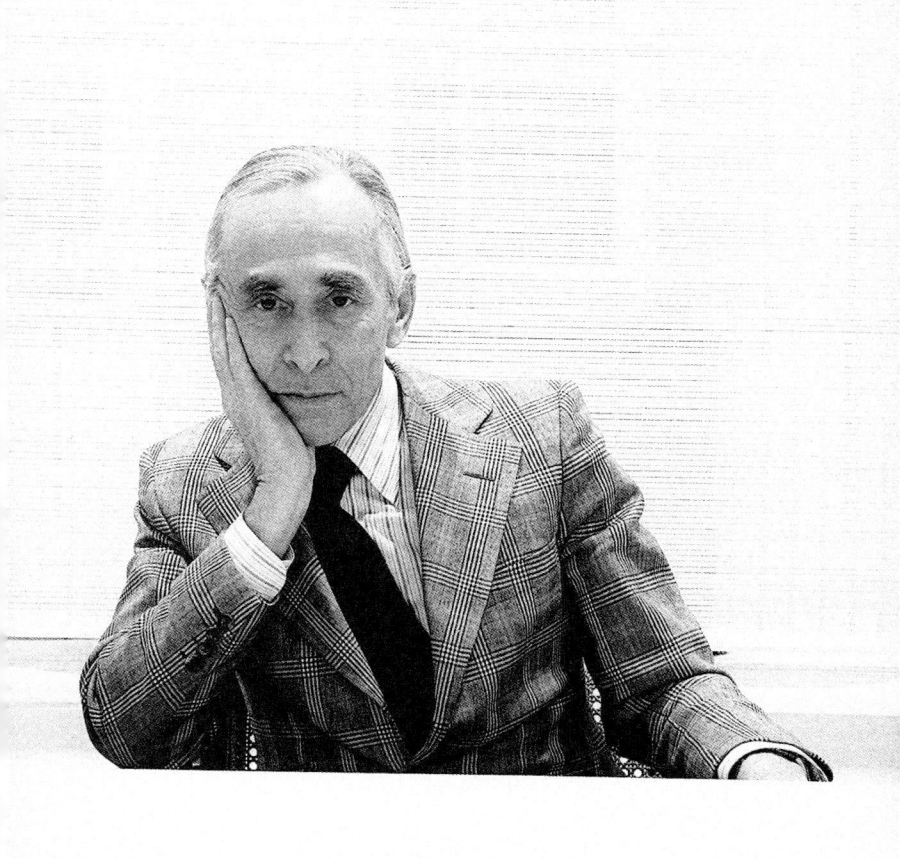

5

EDIE

"I wonder if Edie will commit suicide.
I hope she let's me know so I can film it."
Andy Warhol

When Edie Sedgwick, rich, glamorous, beautiful, vulnerable and tragic (her two brothers had committed suicide) turned up at the Factory, Andy instantly identified his new star. He shot an unscripted movie of her just wandering around, entitled *Poor Little Rich Girl*. They started hanging out, and she accompanied him to parties and openings. She was soon the undisputed queen of the Factory. Andy took her to Paris with him, where he shot her in *Kitchen*. Back in New York he shot her in *Beauty No 1* and *Beauty No 2*. Her boyfriend Bob Neuwirth, part of Bob Dylan's circle, urged her to ditch Warhol (who of course wasn't paying her) and go to Hollywood. Whilst at the Factory, Edie was on amphetamines. When she went to Woodstock with Neuwirth, she got hooked on heroin. She became paranoid, thinking that Andy's movies were making her look a fool. Andy cut her out of his next movie, *My Hustler*. Predictably, Edie was outraged and begged Drella to have her back.

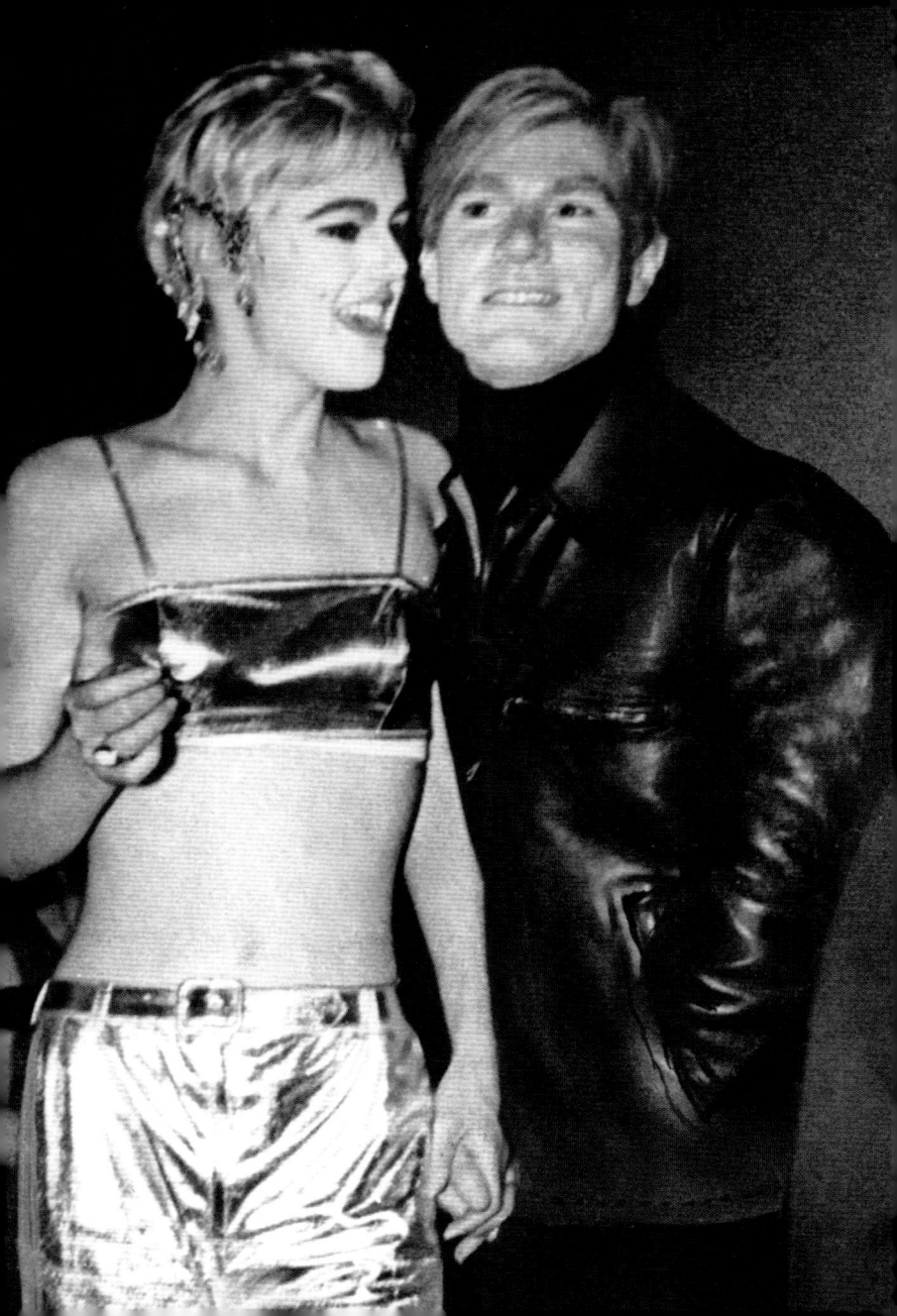

ACTORS AND ARTISTS AT THE FACTORY
...AND WHAT HAPPENED TO THEM.
(ACTORS IN ANDY'S MOVIES IN ITALICS).

DIED TOO YOUNG:
1964 *FREDDIE HERKO*, ACTOR.
SUICIDE FROM FIFTH FLOOR WINDOW, AGED 28.
1968 *ROBERT DRISCOLL*, ACTOR.
HEART FAILURE FROM DRUG ABUSE, AGED 31.
1971 *EDIE SEDGWICK*, ACTRESS AND 'IT' GIRL.
BARBITURATE OVERDOSE, AGED 28.
1972 *ANDREA FELDMAN*, ACTRESS.
SUICIDE FROM 14TH FLOOR WINDOW, AGED 24.
1974 *CANDY DARLIING*, TRANSSEXUAL ACTOR.
LYMPHOMA, AGED 29.
1975 *ERIC EMERSON*, ACTOR.
HIT AND RUN ACCIDENT, AGED 29.
1982 *PAUL AMERICA*, ACTOR
TRAFFIC ACCIDENT, AGED 38.
1985 *JACKIE CURTIS*, ACTOR.
HEROIN OVERDOSE, AGED 38.
1986 *INGRID SUPERSTAR*, ACTRESS.
DISAPPEARED, AGED APPROX 37. PRESUMED DEAD.
1987 ANDY WARHOL, ARTIST AND FILM-MAKER.
VENTRICULAR FIBRILLATION FOLLOWING GALL BLADDER OPERATION, AGED 57.
1988 JEAN-MICHEL BASQUIAT, ARTIST.
HEROIN OVERDOSE, AGED 27.
1988 *PATRICK TILDEN CLOSE*, ACTOR.
ALCOHOLISM, AGED 47.
1988 CHRISTA PÄFFGEN (NICO), SINGER.
HEART ATTACK, AGED 49.

1989 ***ROBERT OLIVO*** (ONDINE), ACTOR.
LIVER DISEASE, AGED 52.
1990 KEITH HARING, ARTIST.
HIV/AIDS, AGED 31.
1993 VICTOR ROJAS, MODEL FOR TORSO SERIES.
HALSTON'S BOYFRIEND. DIED AGED 51.
1996 JED JOHNSON (INTERIOR DESIGNER, BOYFRIEND TO ANDY).
PLANE CRASH, AGED 47.
1986 MARIO AMAYA, ART CRITIC.
HIV/AIDS, AGED 52.
*1988 **VALERIE SOLANAS***, WRITER.
PNEUMONIA, AGED 52.
2002 RICHARD BERNSTEIN, COVER ARTIST, *INTERVIEW*.
HIV/AIDS, AGED 63.
2013 RONNIE CUTRONE, ANDY'S ASSISTANT AND ARTIST.
NATURAL CAUSES, AGED 65.

LONG-LIVED OR HAPPILY STILL AROUND:
BRIGID BERLIN (BRIGID POLK), ACTRESS/ FACTORY MAINSTAY.
LIVING IN NYC.
JOE D'ALLESSANDRO, ACTOR. LIVING IN L.A.
BILLY NAME, PHOTOGRAPHER. DIED AGED 76 IN HUDSON, NY.
BABY JANE HOLZER, ACTRESS.
NOW AN ART COLLECTOR AND FILM PRODUCER.
UDO KIER, ACTOR. LIVING IN PALM SPRINGS, CA.
INTERNATIONAL VELVET, ACTRESS. LIVING IN BOSTON.
MARY WORONOV, ACTRESS. BUSY ACTING CAREER AFTER THE FACTORY,
INCLUDING *CHARLIE'S ANGELS*, *LOGAN'S RUN* AND *CANNONBALL*.

7

PARIS

"The biggest transatlantic fuss since Oscar Wilde brought culture [to the USA]."
New York Herald Tribune

Ileana Sonnabend, one time wife of Leo Castelli, had shown Lichtenstein in Paris and now decided to add Warhol, with his Flowers show, to her stable. She knew Warhol hated flying, and so offered to pay for his sea voyage, but Warhol decided instead to travel by air with Edie, Gerard and Edie's minder, Chuck Wein. It was Andy's first trip to France. The show was a triumph, the critics loved Andy's work. Parisian society just adored Edie and Warhol's style. They were featured as a power couple in *Vogue* and *Paris Match*. The press snapped them at Castel's and Régine's nightclubs. Paris was full of film stars (Peter Sellers, Peter O'Toole, Woody Allen, Ursula Andress and Romy Schneider) as *What's New Pussycat* had just been filmed at Castel's. Picasso, whom Andy admired for being so prolific, sent a note to say how much he liked Andy's work. Andy, perhaps trying to boost his prices, then announced that he planned to stop painting to focus on film.

WHERE?
ANDY'S ENTOURAGE ARRIVING AT ORLY AIRPORT, PARIS.
FROM LEFT: EDIE, ANDY, CHUCK WEIN AND GERARD MALANGA.

70

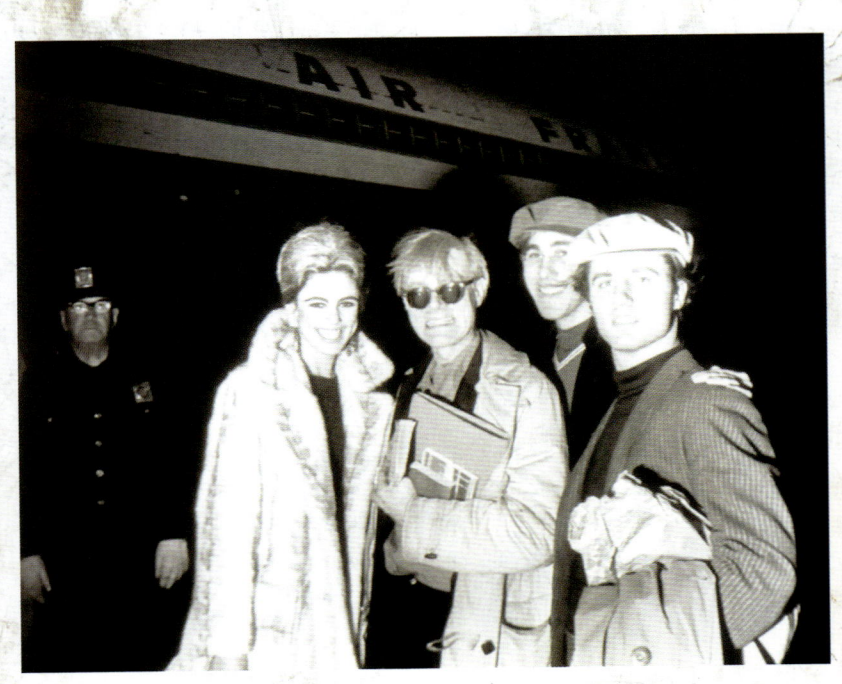

8

THE EXPLODING PLASTIC INEVITABLE

"Andy created multimedia in New York... nothing remained the same after that."
Lou Reed

Andy was now on a high. At the opening of his first US retrospective, in Philadelphia, he and Edie were mobbed like rock stars. Cue the next move. Back in New York, Barbara Rubin introduced Andy to the Velvet Underground, a new band she had seen at Café Bizarre. Andy hit it off with their lead, Lou Reed, and invited the Velvets to the Factory. He also heard that an ice-blonde singer, Nico, was in town, and decided to combine the two. The deal on offer was simple: agree to Nico fronting on some songs, and Andy would manage the Velvets, for 25% of earnings. The first show, The Exploding Plastic Inevitable, with strobes, Andy's movies in the background, and an edgy, up-tight vibe, at The Dom in St Mark's Place, was a sell-out. Everyone was there, including Jackie Kennedy and Marshall McLuhan. Andy had worked his magic: the Velvets achieved instant cult status, and multimedia performance art was born.

WHERE?
ANDY, NICO AND TWO MEMBERS OF THE VELVET UNDERGROUND; PUBLICITY SHOT FOR THE EXPLODING PLASTIC INEVITABLE.

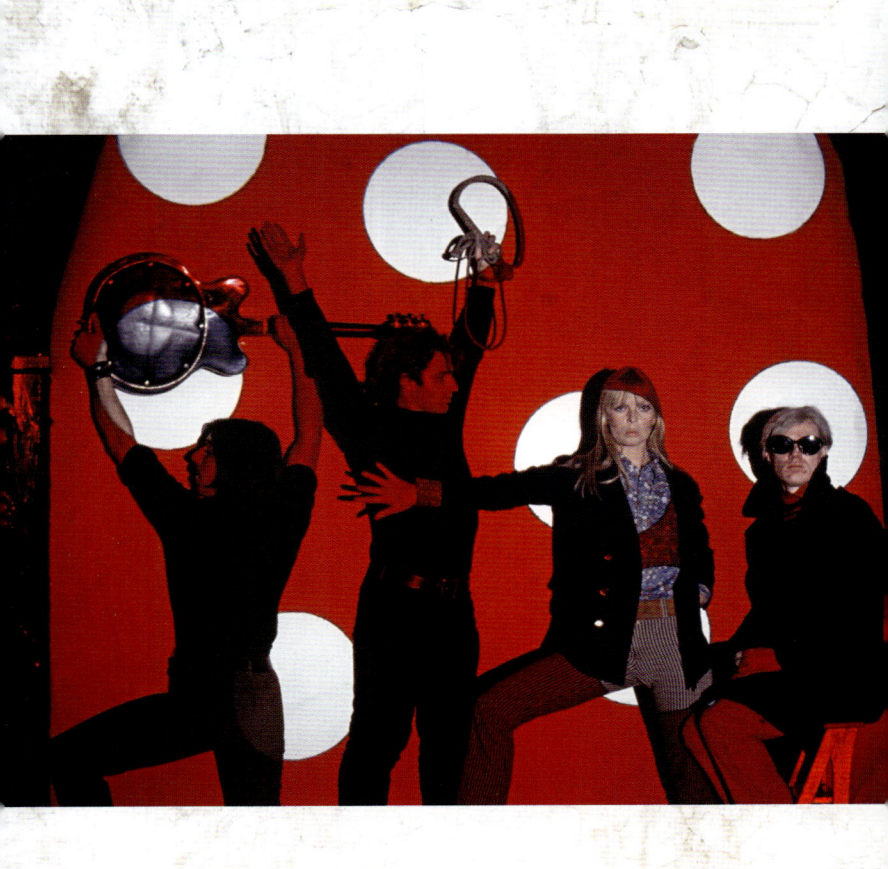

9

THE CHELSEA HOTEL

"About as interesting as the inside of a toilet bowl." Film critic Rex Reid

After a brief show at Castelli's, and having produced the Velvet's first album *Velvet Underground and Nico*, which didn't initially sell well, but went on to become one of the most influential albums ever, Andy focused entirely on film. He would not show at Castelli's again for another 10 years. His movies were starting to turn a profit. He now planned a big movie, designed to be a hit. He started filming the Factory entourage, many of whom lived in the bohemian Chelsea Hotel, in confessional mode, shooting up amphetamine, discussing being gay, stripping off, slagging off other members of the Factory. 15 separate reels were shot, 12 of which were used, often juxtaposed to great effect. It was like reality TV long before its time, a montage of Andy's somewhat sadistic, drug-fuelled and paranoid world. *Chelsea Girls* was a hit, grossing $3 million in today's terms in the first six months. None of the actors were paid. "Be patient," Andy would tell them.

WHAT?
THE STUNNING POSTER, BY LONDON-BASED DESIGNER ALAN ALDRIDGE, ADVERTISING *CHELSEA GIRLS*. ANDY COMMENTED: "I WISH THE MOVIE WERE AS GOOD AS THE POSTER."

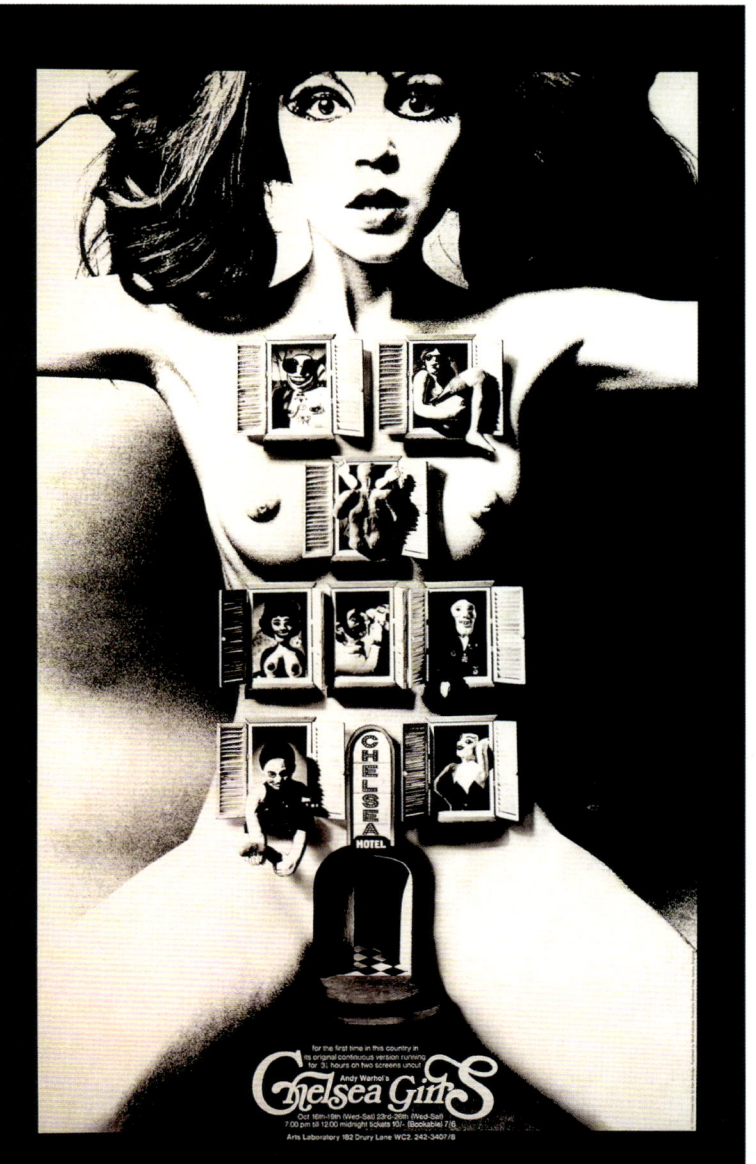

for the first time in this country in
its original continuous version running
for 3½ hours on two screens uncut

Andy Warhol's
Chelsea Girls

Oct 16th–19th (Wed-Sat) 23rd-26th (Wed-Sat)
7.00 pm till 12.00 midnight tickets 10/- (Bookable) 7/6

Arts Laboratory 182 Drury Lane WC2. 242-3407/8

10

MAX'S KANSAS CITY

"The only quasi-assfuck/ pudsuck bar in town to also serve decent food."
Richard Meltzer

As *Chelsea Girls* broke into the mainstream, so the press started to take a negative interest in Andy and what was perceived to be his nihilism and the depravity of the Factory. Andy just let the negativity flow; for him the reaction was all part of the art. He began holding court at Max's, a restaurant/nightclub opened by lawyer Mickey Ruskin. It soon became the centre of the New York art scene. Roy Lichtenstein's crowd used to hold court at the front, whilst Andy and the Factory crowd occupied the outrageous back room. Here Andy ruled the roost most nights from midnight, with Paul Morissey, Brigid Polk and Ronnie Cutrone and whatever 'stars' he had chosen for his movies – Edie Sedgwick, Ultraviolet and Viva amongst them. Casual, boots-only nudity and amphetamines fuelled the party atmosphere. Later, the Velvets would play Max's and Debbie Harry waited tables here. It's epicentre status was maintained throughout the '70s (Jagger and Bowie were regulars), before it closed in 1981.

WHERE?
213 PARK AVENUE SOUTH,
MANHATTAN.

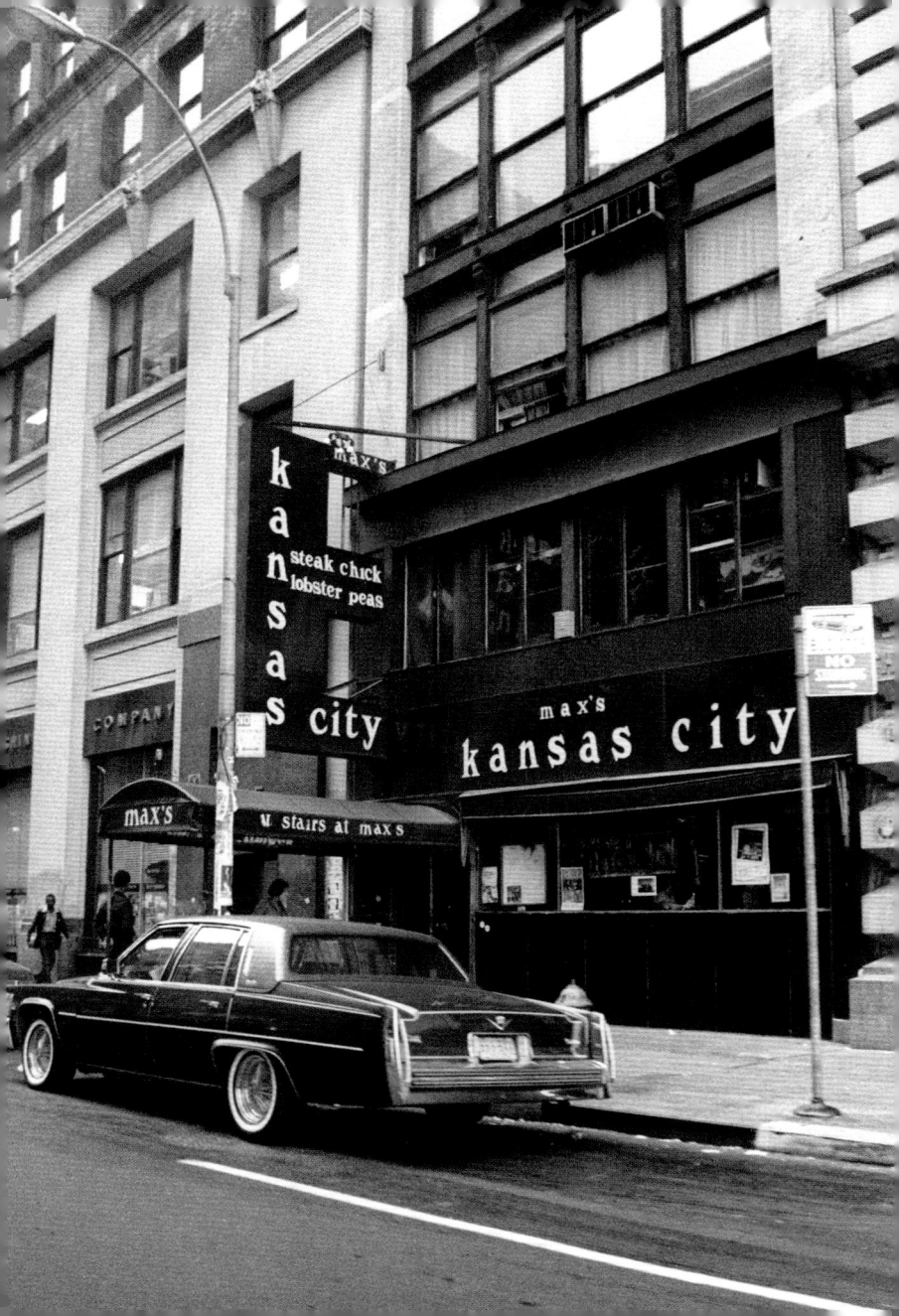

ANDY'S BOYFRIENDS AND LOVE INTERESTS

● Love interest/infatuation of Andy's
● Consummated relationship
● Boyfriend
● Close companion

● RALPH 'CORKIE' WARD

Andy's 'love affair' in 1951. It's unlikely it was consummated.

●● CARL WILLERS

Andy met Carl, his first proper boyfriend, at the New York Public Library in 1953.The relationship lasted a year, but they remained friends.

● CHARLES LISANBY

Andy met Charles, a set designer, in 1954 and fell completely in love. Andy hoped their round the world trip would lead to Charles falling for him physically, but he didn't and they split, but stayed friends until 1962.

● ED WALLOWITCH

Andy met Ed, a photographer, and very active member of the East Village gay scene, in 1956. The relationship fizzled out in 1958.

● UNKNOWN LOVER

Andy had a purely sexual relationship with an unnamed man on the gay scene between 1961-63.

● JOHN GIORNO

John Giorno, a stockbroker, later a talented poet, performance artist and AIDS activist, was 22 when Andy, 34, met him in 1962. John wasn't initially attracted to Andy, but gave in. John loved the Factory scene; Andy used that to manipulate him emotionally. John was the subject of Andy's first film, *Sleep*. The relationship petered out in about 1964. They were back in touch in the mid-'80s.

● PHILIP FAGAN

Andy met Philip in 1964. He began helping out at the Factory, and they became close, with Philip moving in with Andy for a while. Philip moved on in 1965.

● DANNY WILLIAMS

A young Harvard graduate, who became a movie lights-and-sound man, Danny met Andy in late 1965 and moved in with him, but the relationship only lasted two months. Danny then moved into the Factory.

RICHARD GREEN

Andy met the young Richard in San Francisco in 1966 and they began an 'erotic correspondence.' Richard moved into the Lexington Avenue house. Two months later, suspecting Richard was being 'unfaithful,' Andy threw him out.

ROD LA ROD

Only 19 when Andy took up with him at the end of '66. It was a camp, but physical relationship, and Andy took him everywhere, although Rod was only a quasi-boyfriend. In May '67, Andy dumped him.

JED JOHNSON

Jed, Andy's most important relationship, was hired as the floor sweeper at the Factory in 1968, aged 20. He was soon editing some of Warhol's and Morrissey's movies, including *Dracula* and *L'Amour*. Andy and Jed would go on to live together at East 66th Street for 12 years. Jed, now a designer, created the uber-elegant interiors. In 1980 Jed and Andy broke up and Jed moved out. Jed was killed in a plane crash in 1996.

CHRIS MAKOS

Clever, sophisticated Chris Makos, photographer and artist, became close to Warhol in 1980. He and Andy hung out and travelled abroad together.The relationship was partly exhibitionist/voyeuristic: Andy loved to photograph Chris having sex with other men. Andy treated Makos, on-and-off, as a quasi-boyfriend.

JON GOULD

Makos introduced Andy to Jon Gould, an L.A. movie executive, aged 28 to Andy's 53, in 1981. Andy fell totally in love, even though Jon was straight. They travelled together and Jon moved into the East 66th Street house in 1983. Even though the relationship was probably unconsummated, Andy and Jon became very close. In 1984 Jon was diagnosed with AIDS. Andy, with deep ignorance, began asking his maids to wash Jon's clothes separately from his. Jon went back to L.A. in 1985 and died in 1986. He was Andy's last truly close companion.

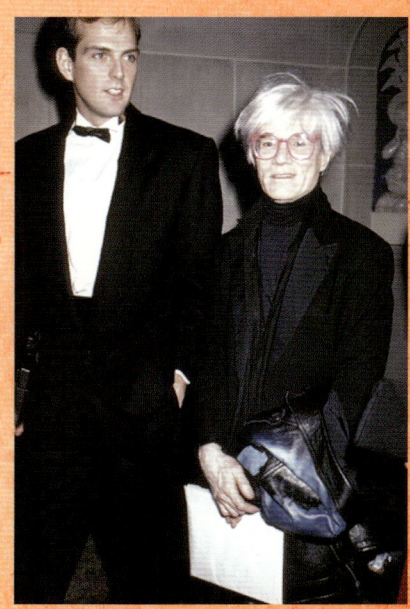

Andy with Jed.

THE NUDE RESTAURANT

"Andy Warhol, get off the stage, you have had your time, you're not really art."
The New York Times

Andy wasn't done with filming yet. *Nude Restaurant* was shot in one day at the Mad Hatter in Manhattan. There were two versions, one where the 'customers' were mostly nude and another, for more general distribution, where they were all in G-strings. The star, playing a monologuing waitress, was Viva. Andy was now moving into quasi-porn, sexploitation movies; he cutely called them 'nudies.' But Viva was smart, a writer who happened to look great on camera. She developed a real talent for publicity. The press's prurient interest in nudity meant that she was getting almost as many column inches as Andy for a while. Andy considered this payment enough – Viva never got a dime. Yet the Factory hangers-on continued to happily perform, in hope of stardom. Andy was indifferent. Two movies he completed – *Imitation of Christ* and *24 Hour Movie* – he withdrew from circulation after just one showing. The actors didn't even get the solace of a little publicity. Meanwhile the press was starting to hate Andy.

WHERE?
MAD HATTER RESTAURANT AND TEA ROOM,
CORNER OF BLEEKER STREET AND 7TH AVENUE, MANHATTAN.

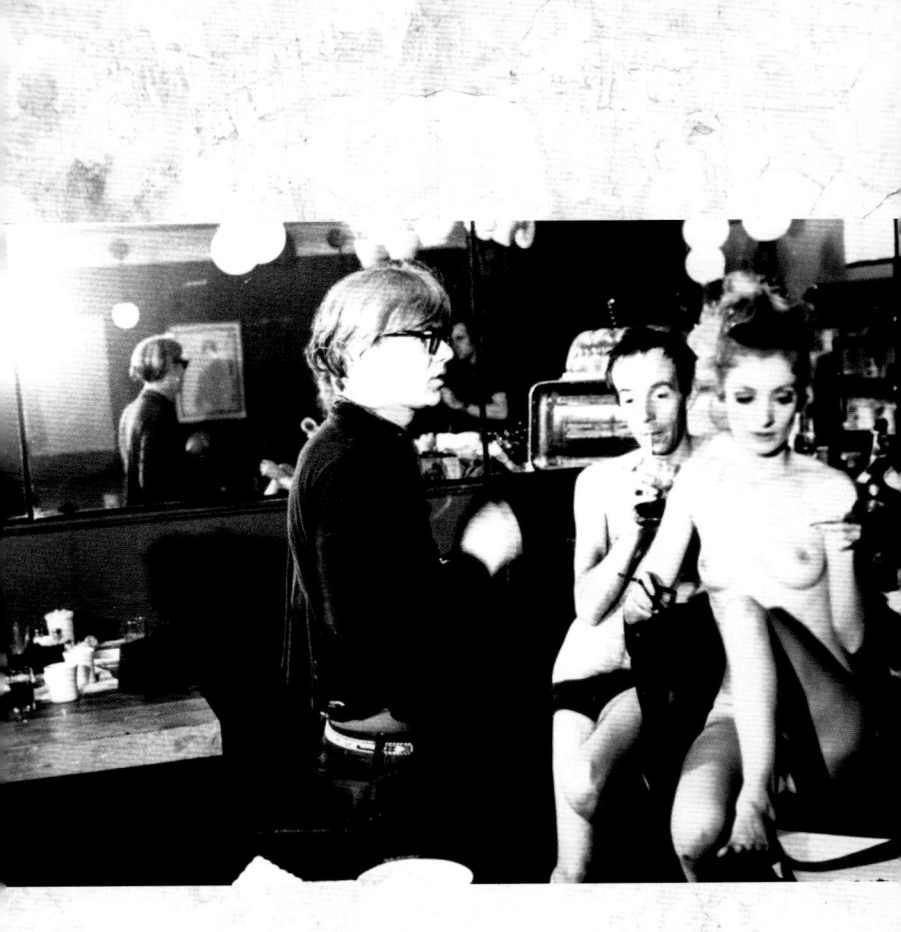

ARIZONA

"You perverted Easterners, go back the hell where you came from."
Arizona locals, shouting at the Factory actors.

It was on the lecture tour that Andy and Paul Morissey thought about shooting a movie in the desert. *Lonesome Cowboys* starred Viva, a rich rancher who got into trouble with a local cowboy gang. Andy took a big risk moving the Factory to redneck country. The local press had been alerted and crowds gathered around the set to make sure that any obscenity was kept at bay. Viva's reputation as a nymphomaniac had preceded her. Some real cowboys did hang around the set, hoping to catch her in the act. The atmosphere on set got poisonous; at points the anger between the actors was no longer feigned, but real. A scene of simulated rape with Viva was rumoured to have turned into actual rape. The FBI were informed and opened a file on Andy, which they maintained, watching his every move, for over a year. Eventually cast and crew were, as in a real Western, hounded out of town, and Andy finished the film in New York. It was the last film he would personally direct: easier to let Paul do them in future, he decided.

WHAT?
THE POSTER FOR THE US RELEASE OF
LONESOME COWBOYS.

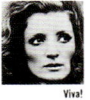 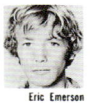 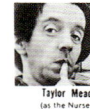
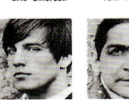 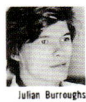
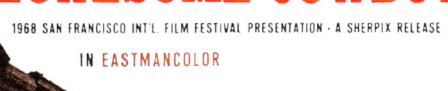
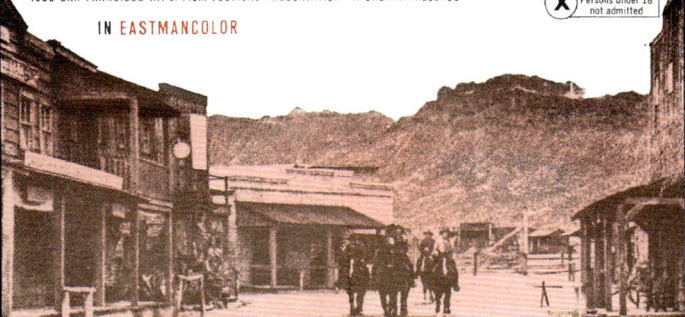

14

THE FACTORY (NO. 2)

"There were all these people hanging around hoping to find themselves, but losing themselves more and more."
Benedetta Barzini, Vogue model.

With Fred Hughes increasingly in the picture, and the lease on the first Factory coming up for renewal, Andy decided it was time to move. Almost in anticipation of a change of vibe, he chose the sixth floor of the smart Decker Building on Union Square. Hughes tried to instill, with only limited success, a more business-like, less party-like, mood. There were two large rooms. At the front was the designated office/ exhibition space, with white walls, a polished wooden floor, IBM typewriters and white phones on black glass-topped desks. At the back was the painting and film screening space. Morissey was now put in charge of new movies. Andy was beginning to detach himself from Factory cast members.

WHERE?
THE DECKER BUILDING,
33 UNION SQUARE WEST,
MANHATTAN.

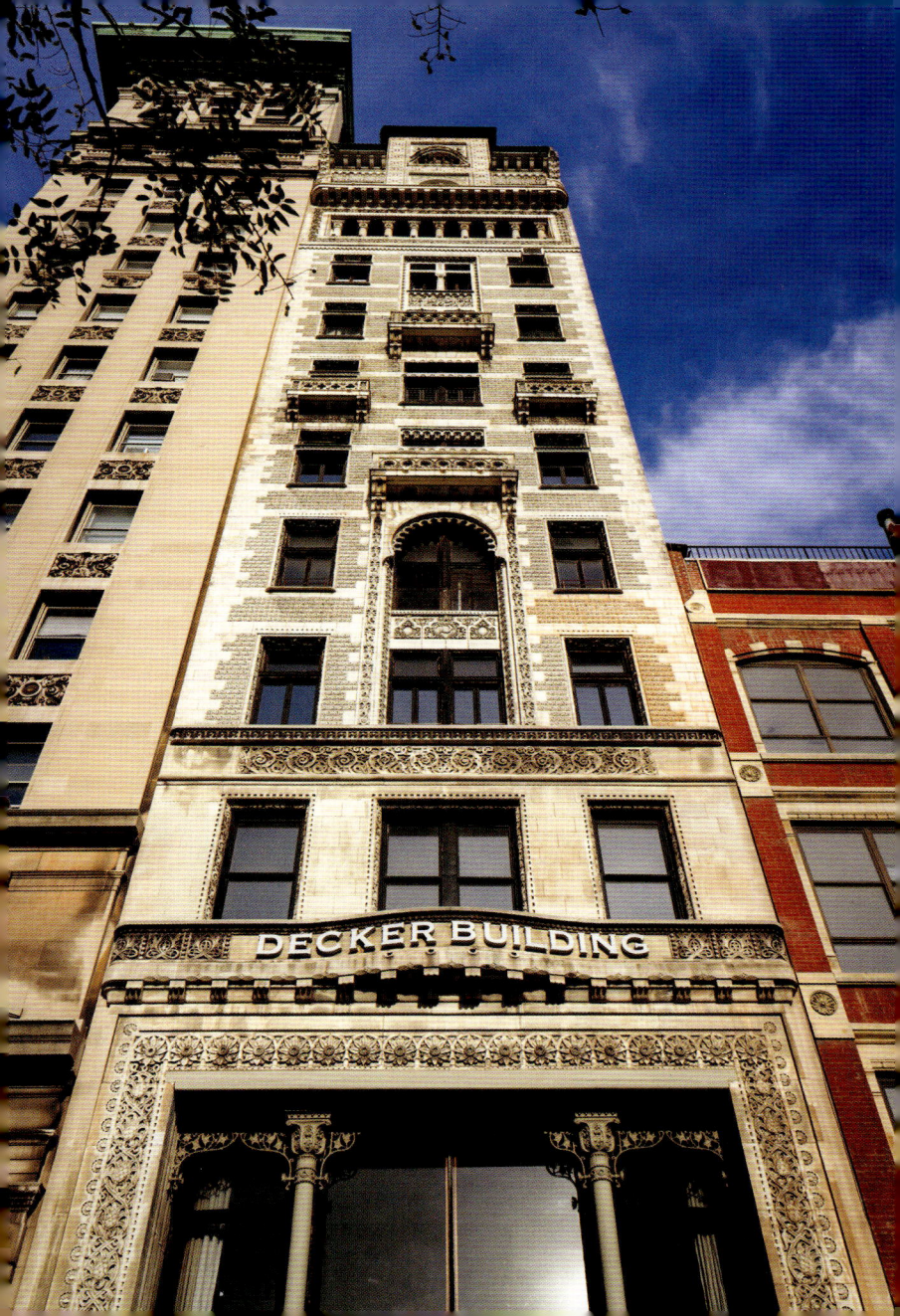

THE SHOOTING

"Felled by scum."
Time magazine

Valerie Solanas, lesbian and women's lib activist, had acted in Andy's *I, a Man*, in 1967. She had also invited Warhol to film a script she had written, *Up Your Ass*. Andy, in his usual way, had said 'sure,' but when he proceeded to lose the script, she developed an exaggerated, paranoid grudge. A few months later, on Monday 3rd June, 1968, Valerie came to the Factory looking for Andy. She waited out on the street until he turned up in the afternoon. They travelled up in the lift together. Andy wandered over to sit at one of the desks, ignoring Solanas. She reached into her coat, pulled out a .32 automatic and fired. No one quite grasped what had happened, except Andy. He screamed. She fired again. Andy crawled under the desk. She fired again. The bullet entered Andy's right side, and exited his back on the left. Blood seeped everywhere. Solanas then shot Mario Amaya, and then turned her attention on Fred Hughes: "Please don't shoot...please just leave." Valerie seemed to move away, then returned and aimed at Fred's forehead and pulled the trigger. The gun jammed. Only then did she bolt for the elevator and flee. Andy, his lung punctured by the bullet, lay dying on the floor.

WHAT?
DAILY NEWS FRONT PAGE, JUNE 4TH, 1968.

DAILY NEWS
NEW YORK'S PICTURE NEWSPAPER ®

Vol. 49. No. 296 Copr. 1968 News Syndicate Co. Inc.   New York, N.Y. 10017, Tuesday, June 4, 1968*   WEATHER: Sunny and warm.

ACTRESS SHOOTS ANDY WARHOL

Cries 'He Controlled My Life'

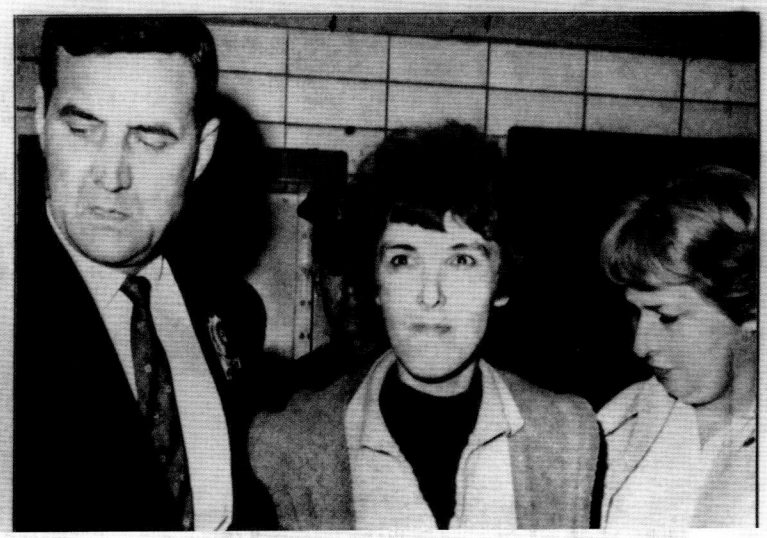

16

THE E.R.

"A $1,000 cheque and can of soup prints: Andy Warhol's gift to doctor who saved his life." The Times

Nothing was the same again. Andy had been shot at around 4:22pm. The ambulance arrived at 4.35 pm. He was wheeled into the emergency room at 4.45pm. At 4.51pm Andy was pronounced clinically dead in the ER. But his surgeon, Dr Giuseppe Rossi, didn't give up so easily. He and his team operated to repair the damage to his lung, spleen, oesophagus, intestine, gall bladder and liver. It took five and a half hours. His chances of survival were now estimated to be 50/50. Andy slowly improved and, on June 13th, his doctors declared he would make a full recovery. He was moved to a private room and given another lifeline – a telephone. Andy went home, finally, on July 28th. He spent the whole of August there. He now had to permanently wear a surgical corset. His doctors said he could no longer take Obetrol. Andy declared to the press that he was scared. They tried to blame him for Solanas's actions (a result of the depraved games at the Factory, they suggested). Slowly he began turning up at the Factory for a few hours each day, but would be tucked up at home by 8pm every night. Meanwhile, the price of Warhol paintings shot up.

WHERE?
THE AMBULANCE OUTSIDE THE UNION SQUARE FACTORY, WAITING FOR ANDY TO BE BROUGHT DOWN ON A STRETCHER. ART CRITIC MARIO AMAYA, WHO WAS ALSO SHOT (THE BULLET LUCKILY ONLY GRAZED HIS BACK) LOOKS ON.

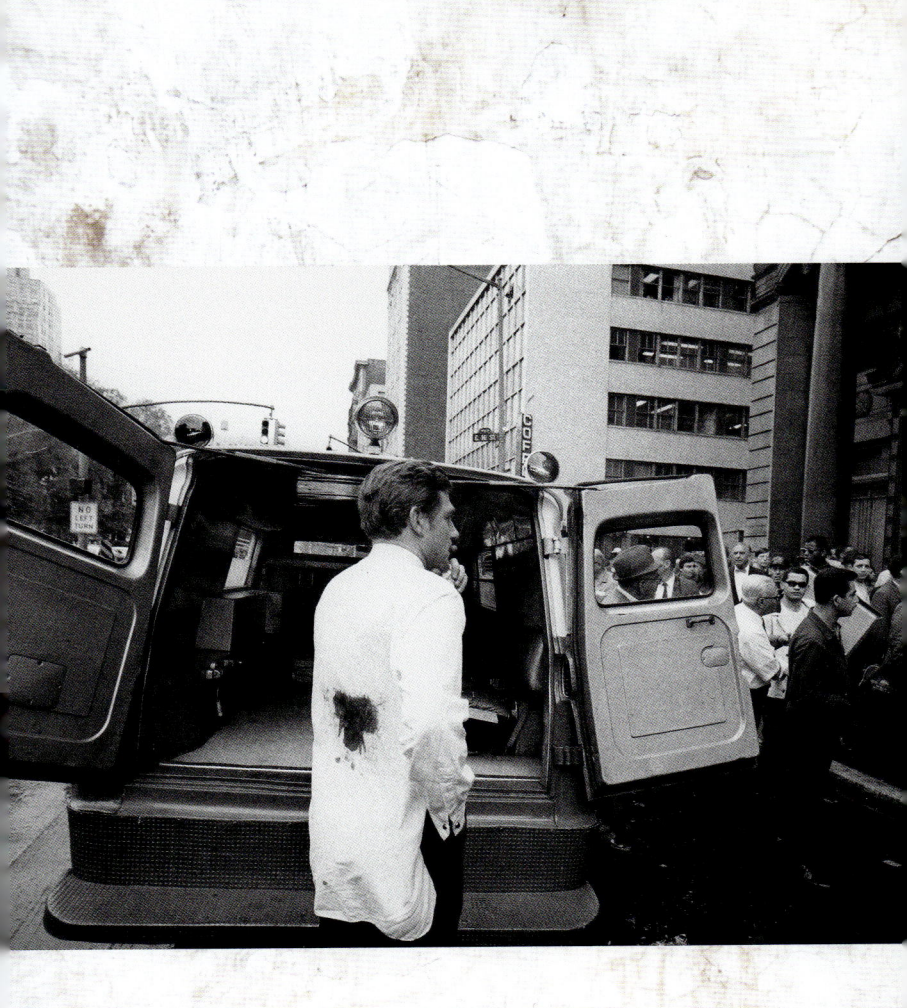

ANDY'S MANHATTAN 1961-1987

As Andy's wealth grew, so more of his life began to gravitate around the Upper East Side. He moved 25 blocks closer to The Plaza from the Lex house in 'Little Hungary,' to the much smarter 57, E66th Street, where his neighbours were the uber wealthy old money set and assorted dictators and their wives. Halston's party pad and Studio 54 were close. But work, and some of the edgier play, remained firmly downtown. Andy would take a cab into the Factory most days. When he did go to his compound in Montauk, he would take the seaplane (flights in modern values around $750 each way) from the East River at 23rd Street.

KEY
🔴 Locations of the Factory
🟠 Andy's House
🔵 Other significant locations

LOCATIONS:

1 Factory No 1:
231 East 47th St

2 Factory No 2:
Decker Building,
33 Union Sq West

3 Factory No 3:
860 Broadway (north end of Union Sq)

4 Factory No 4:
22 East 33rd St

HOUSES:

1 1342 Lexington Ave

2 57 East 66th St

3 Montauk, Long Island, site of Andy's Eothen compound

OTHER:

1 The Chelsea Hotel:
204 West 23rd St

2 Max's Kansas City:
213 Park Ave South

3 The Mad Hatter:
Bleeker St and 7th Ave

4 Serendipity:
225 East 58th St

5 The Dom:
St Mark's Place

6 The Halston House:
101 East 63rd St

7 The Church of St Vincent Ferrer: 869 Lexington Ave

8 The Empire State Building: 20 West 34th St

9 The Castelli Gallery 1:
East 77th St

10 The Castelli Gallery 2 (from 1971):
420 West Broadway, Soho

11 Studio 54:
254 West 54th St

12 The Mudd Club:
77 White St, Tribeca.

13 The Anvil gay BDSM club: 500 West 14th St

14 The Mineshaft gay BDSM club: 835 Washington St

15 23rd St Seaplane base

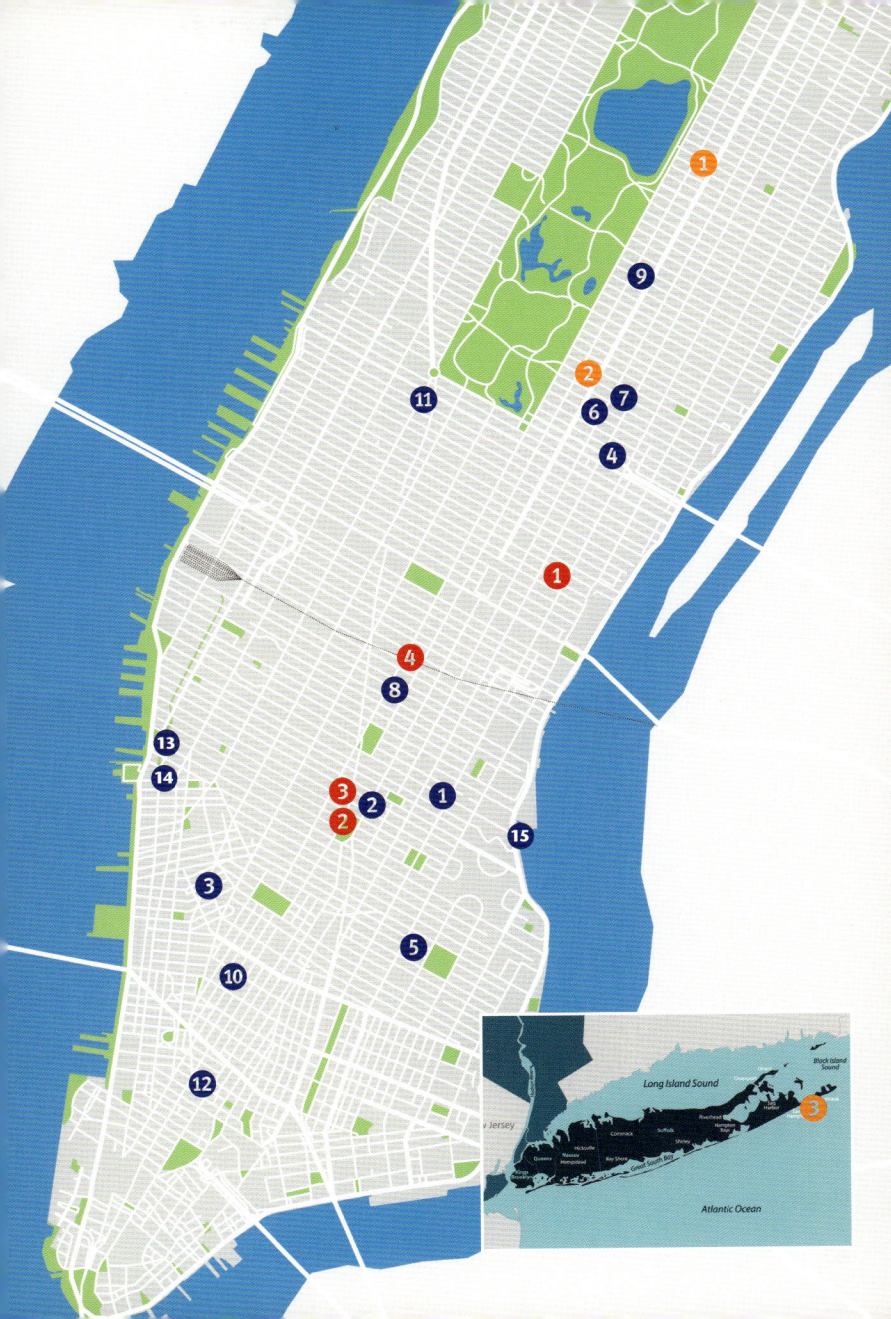

Andy Warhol probably wasn't the first person to use what became his most famous statement:

"IN THE FUTURE EVERYONE WILL BE WORLD-FAMOUS FOR 15 MINUTES"

"We've decided it's by Warhol, whether he likes it or not."
Blake Gopnik, art critic

WHERE WAS THE PHRASE FIRST USED: The brochure for Andy's first solo museum exhibition in Europe, at the Moderna Museet, Stockholm.

WHEN: September 1968

SO WHO SAID IT?

Does it matter? It has become Andy's and it took Andy to make it famous. Nat Finkelstein, a photographer, may have suggested it to Andy in 1966, and others think it was Pontus Hultén, the curator of the Moderna Museet.

DID ANDY SUBSEQUENTLY USE IT?

Yes! *Andy Warhol's Fifteen Minutes* was a US talk show on MTV which ran from 1985 until 1987. The first episode was opened by co-host Debbie Harry with the themes of Sex, Vegetables, Brothers and Sisters. Warhol played the role of the shy main host, with his awkward but probing questions. It was cult viewing.

1969-1971

Andy recalibrated after the shooting. He became less of a party animal. Just as *Vogue* was now calling him 'the most famous artist in America', *Esquire* was declaring that the avant-garde was over, showing Andy drowning in a tin of Campbell's soup on its cover. But the movies started to make money and the museum world now recognised Andy as an important artist, a definer of the age. His prices started climbing fast. Then in 1970, the young Fred Hughes stepped in to run Andy Warhol Enterprises. "I could make you seriously rich" he told Andy, and he did. Fred encouraged Andy to get back to painting, and introduced the idea of the celebrity portrait. Andy now started moving amongst the international, hyper-wealthy jet-set: Hollywood stars, rock aristocracy, the Agnellis, Niarchoses, de Menils, Yves Saint Laurent and Paloma Picasso. He also capitalised on his growing reputation in Europe. In Germany his movie *Trash* was a major success. Andy's look now changed: velvet jackets and bespoke shirts replaced the biker jackets and t-shirts.

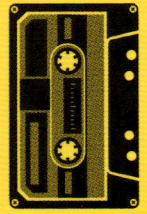

Andy and his Casette Recorder
Just as Andy was recording the banality of everyday consumer objects – Coke, Campbell's soup – so he hit upon the idea of recording conversations and photographing (on his Minox 35EL) or filming people just 'being'. Andy acquired the first consumer casette recorder, the Norelco Carry-Corder EL3300–150 (not quite as grabby a name as Walkman...), and began recording the amphetamine-fuelled ramblings of Factory regulars. "Art just wasn't fun for me anymore...it was people who were fascinating...listening to them, and making movies of them", he declared. He soon began carrying his recorder by its shoulder strap everywhere, affectionately referring to it as "my wife".

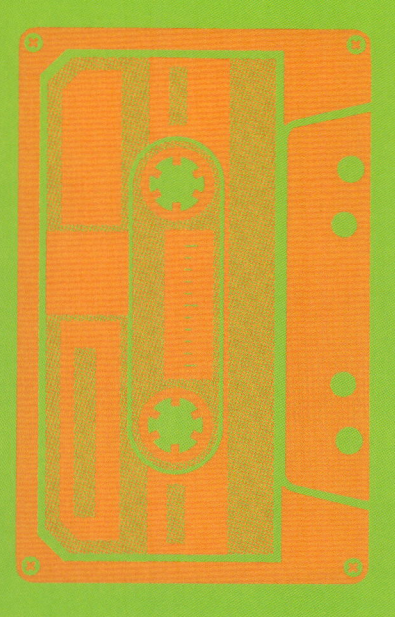
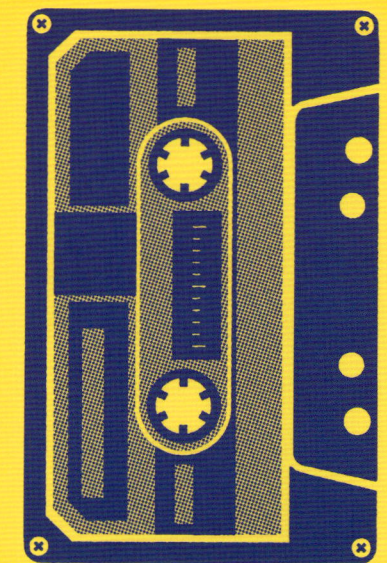
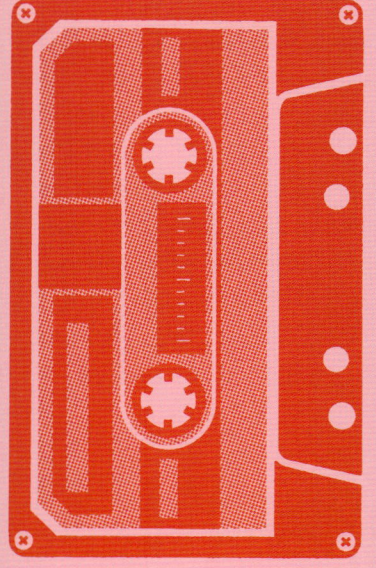
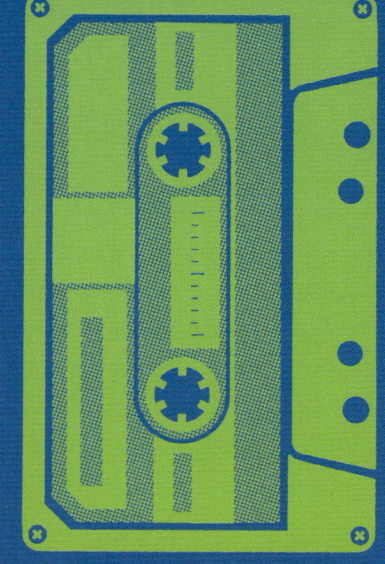

ESQUIRE

"Some would maintain Andy Warhol's greatest artwork is 'Andy Warhol'."
Vogue

Andy was now in a funk. One of his few new ideas was to photograph, with his polaroid, the cock and balls of anyone who turned up at the Factory. Part of the fun was guessing who would say 'yes.' Andy collected thousands of cock polaroids. It was all starting to feel quite jaded, hence the story that *Esquire* ran in their May 1969 issue. But the Factory was still churning out movies, including *Blue Movie*, *Flesh* and *Trash*. The last proved a major hit. It cost, in today's terms, around $300,000 to produce, but would go on to make $15 million. *Blue Movie* and *Flesh* had a tougher time. The former was declared obscene and seized by the NYPD. A showing of *Flesh* in London led to the whole audience being arrested. Yet, whilst creatively Andy may have dried up, the museum world was newly keen on Andy. A major retrospective of his work was planned for Pasadena, Chicago, Eindhoven (Holland), Paris, London and the Whitney in New York. Warhol was still relevant.

WHAT?
FRONT COVER OF *ESQUIRE*, MAY 1969,
SUGGESTING ANDY WAS A SPENT FORCE.

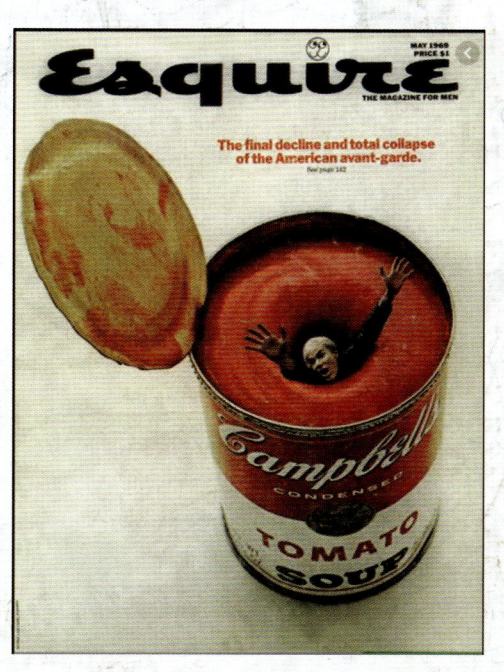

FRED HUGHES

"Fred engineered the rise of Andy Warhol from the demimonde to the beau monde."
Bob Colacello

Andy had met the sharp, smart Fred Hughes, then aged 22, at a party of Philip Johnson's at his Glass House in 1967. They instantly got each other. Prices for Warhol paintings were then heading south, despite his notoriety, but Fred scented that the situation could be turned around. "I could make you properly wealthy", he told Warhol. Andy loved the fact that Fred was a protégé of the super-moneyed de Menil family, so Fred joined the Factory, soon becoming Andy's business manager. After the shooting things started to snowball. Fred developed the idea of commissioned portraits. He understood the mindset of the super-rich, so Andy had to be expensive: $25,000 a go. The de Menils became Warhol patrons, buying the 'unsaleable' *Death and Disaster* series, and then commissioning portraits. In his Everall Brothers suits and John Lobb shoes, Fred slid easily into high society, and introduced Warhol to the set that included Halston, Mick and Bianca Jagger, Jack Nicholson and Diana Vreeland.

WHERE?
FRED HUGHES WITH PALOMA PICASSO,
AT A PARTY FOR YVES SAINT LAURENT.

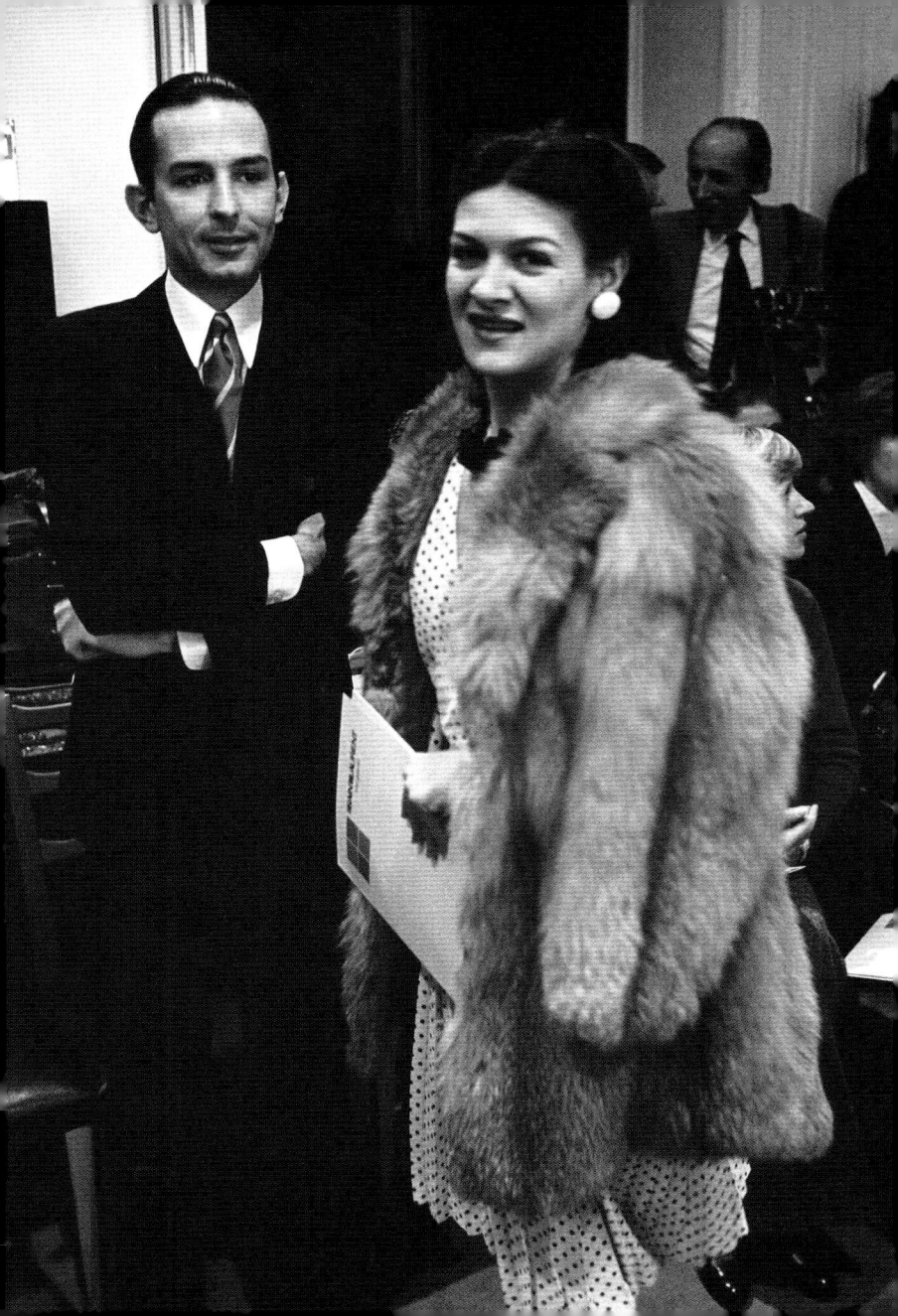

HOLLYWOOD

"If only someone would give us a million dollars..." Andy Warhol

Andy loved Hollywood and he recognised its power. He had bankrolled most of his own movies, but now he wanted a big studio to really back him. There was no question that Andy had created movies with more than niche market appeal and *Lonesome Cowboys* had just won the San Francisco Film Festival Award. Some of his screwed-up stars were also potentially bankable and under Paul Morissey, Factory movies were becoming more professional. He was working on a treatment with an L.A. reporter and Columbia Pictures were interested enough to fly Andy, Paul and a bevy of Factory regulars out to L.A., putting them up at the luxurious Beverly Wilshire. Columbia fêted them at various nightclubs before the big meeting. Andy sat there inscrutably and let Paul do all the talking. The vibe was disconcerting. The drugs were problematic. They were just too cool for Hollywood. Andy decided that they'd been flown out just to be put down. After four days he pulled everyone home. Hollywood and Warhol were not destined to work together it seemed, although Warhol's life would eventually get the Hollywood treatment, and many directors would be influenced by the Factory's film output.

WHERE?
BEL AIR, WITH THE HOLLYWOOD SIGN IN THE DISTANCE.

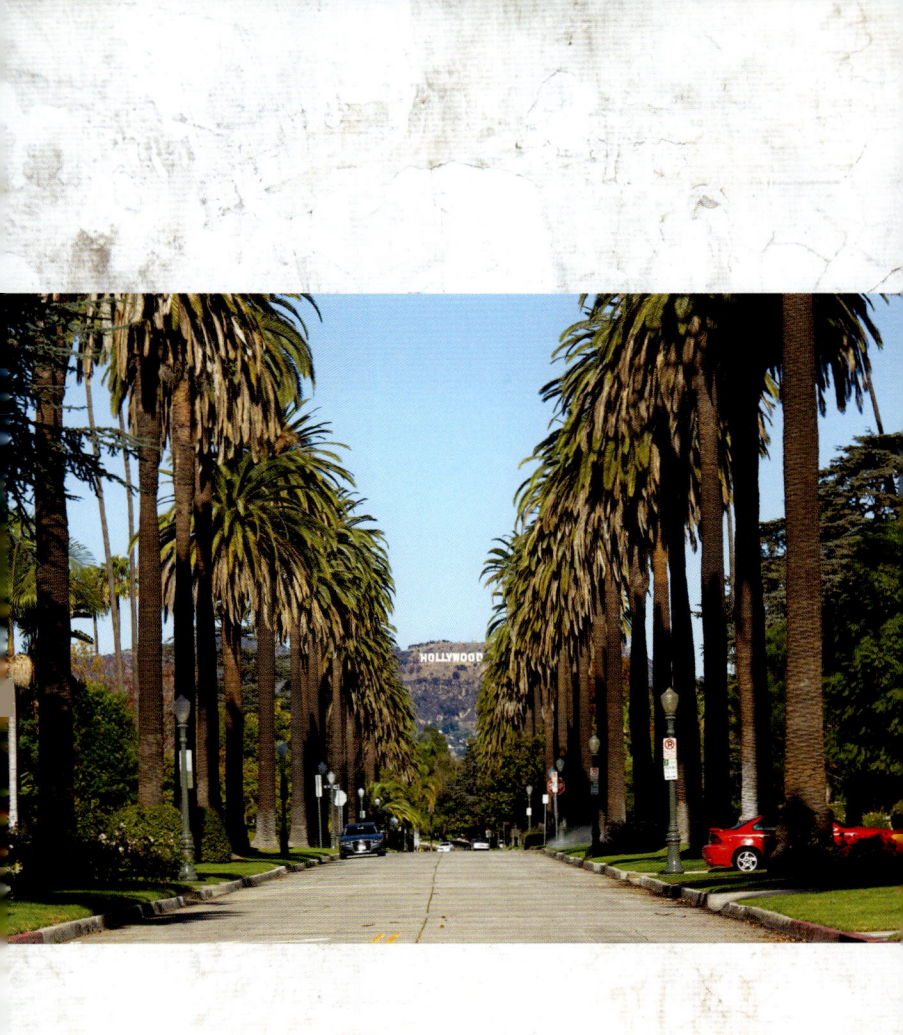

ANDY WARHOL ENTERPRISES

"The new art is really a business."
Andy Warhol

Hollywood may not have taken to Andy, but the mainstream art world was now all over him. In May 1970 one of Andy's Campbell's soup-can paintings fetched $60,000 at auction at Parke Bernet, then the highest price for a living American artist. Fred had been busy on both sides of the Atlantic. Warhols started fetching record prices in Europe also. There was particular demand for the 'unsaleable' *Death and Disaster* series. Andy, who never really believed in art being art, loved the fact that his art was becoming a business. Under Fred, Andy Warhol Enterprises (AWE) took off. He introduced the idea of prints, of the flower series, to be sold through Castelli, ensuring pumped-up prices for not much effort. The de Menils encouraged their friends to commission portraits – Philip Johnson included. Andy even appeared in a hilarious commercial for Braniff airlines, with the strapline "When you got it, flaunt it." He was still very tight with money, but, encouraged by Fred, he began serious collecting. With *objets* it was Art Deco and First Nations American art. With painting, surprisingly, Alma Tadema and Bouguereau. And he also started buying buildings on the Lower East Side, at bargain prices. Fred's influence really was making Andy rich.

WHERE?
FRED (STANDING MIDDLE) WITH ANDY (WITH POLAROID) AT A PARTY IN PARIS, 1970.

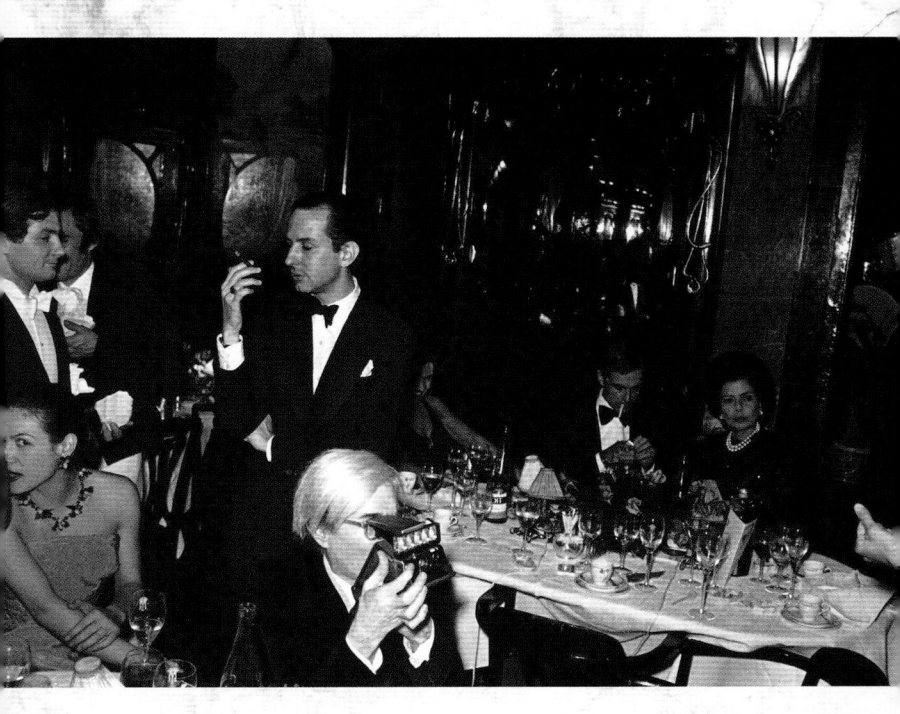

103

LONDON

"Andy was venerated by both the social and art world establishments."
Bob Colacello

In 1971, the first big show of Andy's paintings was held at the Tate. Andy was there for the press reception, and to get *Trash* past the censor. In London he met with Hockney (a favourite of the Queen Mother's), Germaine Greer, Lord Lambton and the Guinnesses. There would soon be a change back at the Factory, where some of the old guard would be replaced by interns from pukka English families (Andy was becoming increasingly anglophile), including Catherine Guinness; they were nicknamed 'the English muffins.' After a short trip to Germany he returned to London for a party held by Tory MP, Norman St John-Stevas, in the House of Commons. Andy's notoriety (the druggy Factory, the 'obscene' movies) was no barrier to Andy moving seamlessly from edginess to the centre of the British Establishment. Andy loved high society and the uber-wealthy. In interviews, only half jokingly, he began to refer to himself as 'a travelling society portrait painter.' The show at the Tate was, predictably, a huge success.

WHERE?
THE HOUSE OF COMMONS,
PALACE OF WESTMINSTER, LONDON.

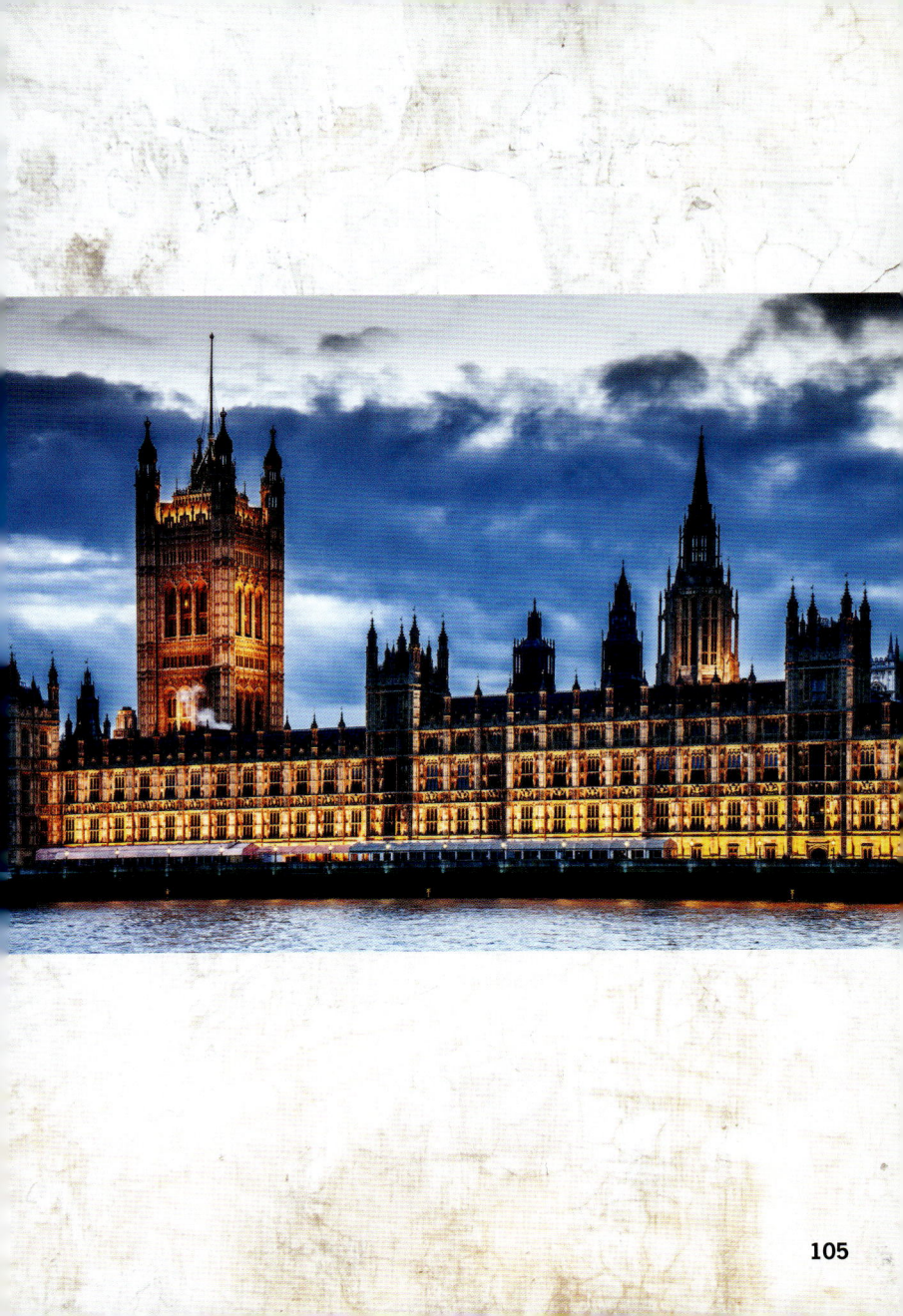

6

MUNICH

"Andy...more like a popular monarch than a pop artist." **Village Voice**

Andy left London quickly to attend the German premiere of *Trash* in Munich. This was Andy's first visit to West Germany. He was already a cult figure there, both for his underground movies (the post-war atmosphere may have helped) and his art, which featured in a number of significant collections. West Germany had fallen in love with pop art long before the USA. It was the Darmstadt Museum, rather than MOMA, that had the world's largest pop art collection; Andy's subversive spirit appealed to left-wing intellectuals, who admired his edge-of-taste movies; the art establishment adored the freshness and wit of his paintings: they seemed to capture the zeitgeist of modernity. *Trash* was a mass-market success in West Germany; with an audience of three million, it made serious money. The main Munich newspaper *Abendzeitung* gave it a best film of 1971 award, and named its star, Joe Dallesandro, best actor.

WHERE?
ANDY LANDING WITH JANE FORTH, LEADING
ACTRESS IN *TRASH*, AT MUNICH AIRPORT, 1971.

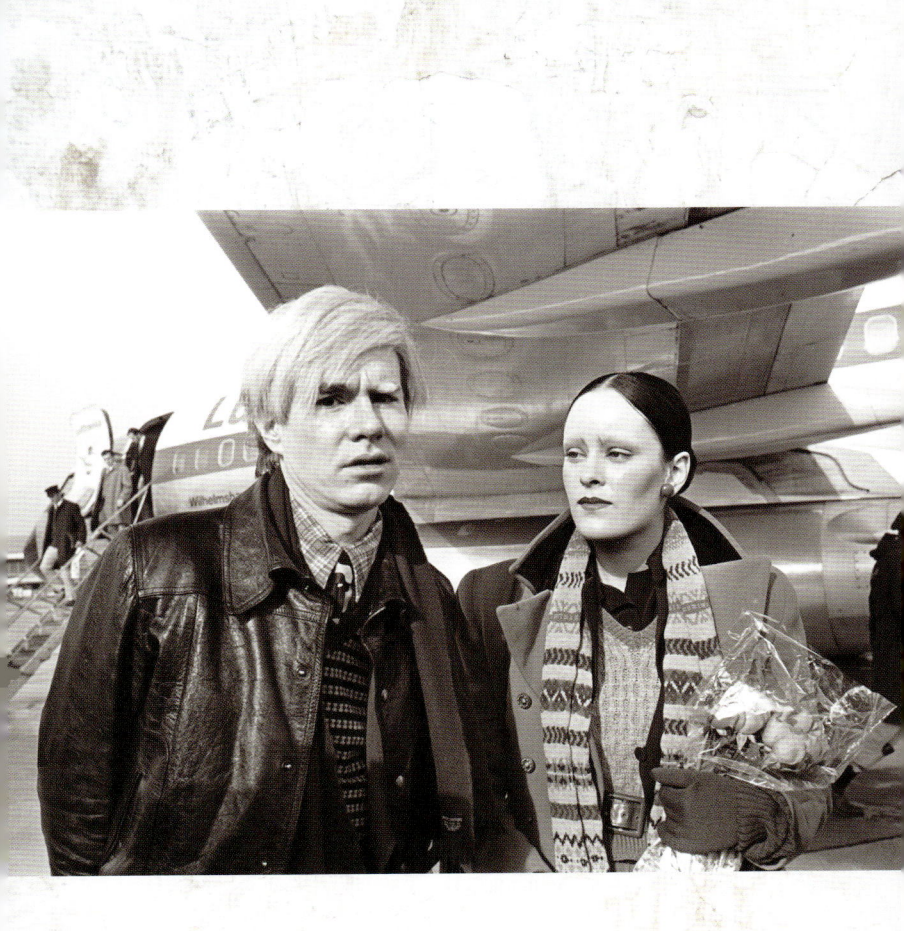

7

LONDON: PORK

"Occasionally revolting but more often good, dirty fun..."
New York Times review of *Pork*.

Andy had the idea of a theatre production based on all the private phone conversations he had been taping of Factory regulars. He handed over the tapes to Tony Zanetta and asked him to turn them into a play. The main character 'Pork' was based on Brigid Polk; 'Vulva Lips' was Viva; the 'Pepsodent twins,' with their pastel-powdered cocks, were based on Jed and Jay Johnson; Andy was B. Marlowe, a voyeur in a wheelchair with his Polaroid at the ready. It was great satire, Andy essentially laughing at the members of the Factory. Most of the actors were naked, variously discussing masturbation, defecation, fucking, farting, abortions, orgasms, threesomes and douching. It only ran in New York for two weeks before transferring to London, at the Roundhouse. It caused a predictable storm of outrage and was a sell-out. David Bowie went to see it three times, partied with the cast, and eventually hired a few to run his management company, MainMan, in New York. It was Andy's only play. One was probably enough.

WHAT?
PORK PERFORMANCE IN LONDON.
LOOKING BACK IS CHERRY VANILLA (KATHLEEN DORRITIE).

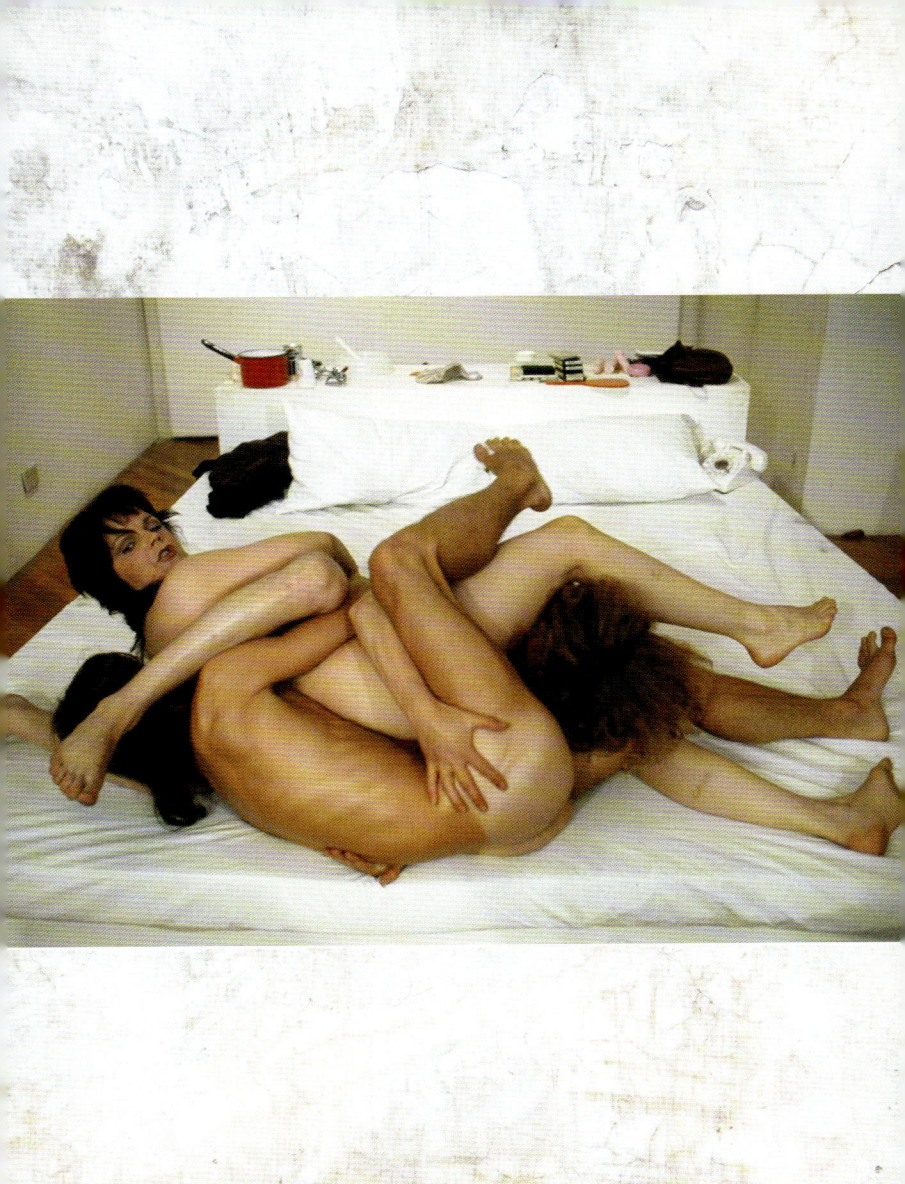

8

BOWIE AND JAGGER

"Fucking voyeur."
Mick's jocular comment on Andy

Andy liked to intimate that Bowie got a lot of his gender-bending ideas for Ziggy from him. That was a bit of a stretch, but Bowie was obsessed with the Warhol phenomenon, writing his song *Andy Warhol* before he met him in New York in 1971. The meeting wasn't a success. Bowie went on to work with the Velvets (producing *Walk on the Wild Side*) and he and Andy would cross paths at various clubs. Andy didn't earn a dime from his album with the Velvets – royalties were never paid, but he still wanted to be part of the rock scene. If Bowie was making money from glitter rock, why couldn't he? The Rolling Stones were the obvious target. Andy had contributed an idea for their album *Through the Past, Darkly* (it was rejected, then, according to Andy, used without permission). He did design the brilliant zipper cover for *Sticky Fingers* (Jed modelled the erection beneath the jeans, Glenn O'Brien the jockey shorts) and then created the best rock 'n' roll logo ever – the red 'lapping tongue,' modelled on Mick's lips. Mick dismissed Andy as a 'fucking voyeur,' but Andy did get to meet Bianca Jagger. He became her favourite artist and they became lifelong friends.

WHERE?
ANDY AND MICK AT THE LAUNCH PARTY FOR
STONES ALBUM *LOVE YOU LIVE*, AT TRAX,
MANHATTAN.

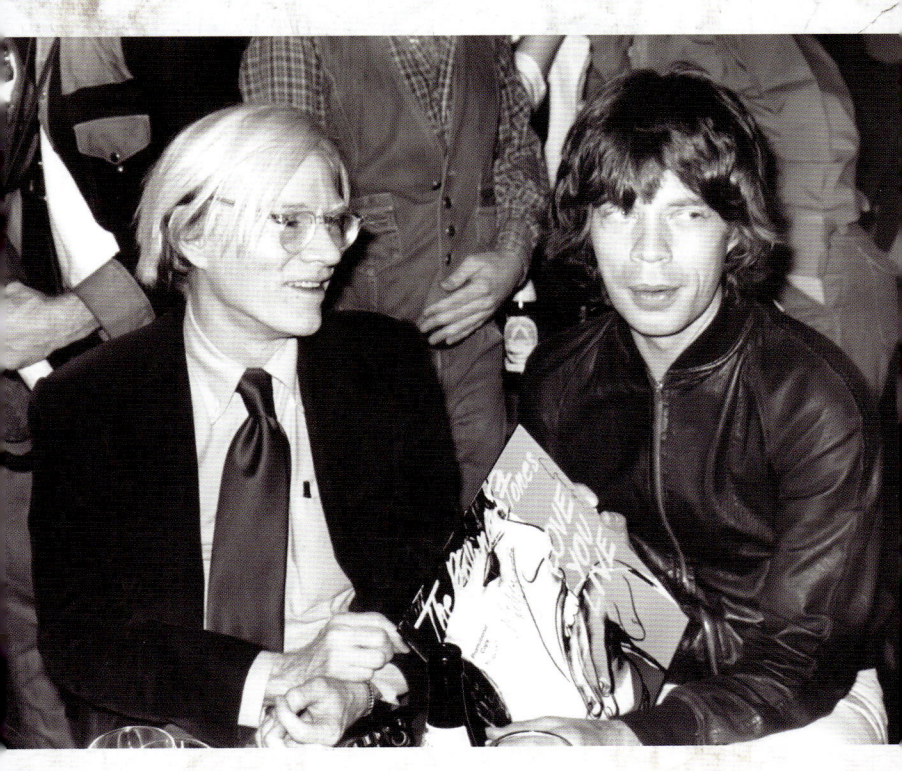

EOTHEN, MONTAUK

"I dread going there. I hate the sun. I hate the sea. I hate slipping between those damp wet sticky sheets." **Andy Warhol**

Andy and Paul Morissey were in the Hamptons in August 1971, editing a new movie, *Heat*, and somehow ended up together buying this 30-acre ocean-front estate, with its six cottages, at the eastern tip of Long Island, for $225,000 ($900,000 in today's terms). Andy's declared intention was to have a refuge away from the social whirl of Manhattan. In fact, he rarely went, choosing instead to rent it to members of his set, in particular Bianca, who would of course invite him out. In 1974 the Rolling Stones all turned up to rehearse there, giving Montauk instant notoriety. Tons of groupies came in their wake. Warhol as the celebrity catalyst was once again performing his magic. Other guests included Jackie O., Liz Taylor, Liza Minnelli and John Lennon. Morissey inherited Andy's portion on his death, and held onto it until 2007, when he sold up for $27 million. The estate was on the market again in 2015, for $85 million.

WHERE?
MONTAUK,
LONG ISLAND,
NEW YORK STATE.

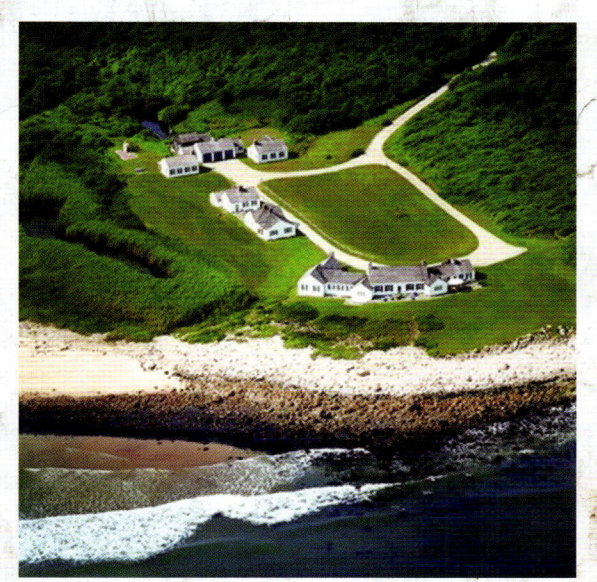

MAO ZEDONG

"The most famous person in the world today is Mao." **Life magazine, 1972**

1972 was momentous. Nixon had gone to China and Andy decided to return, much to Fred's relief, to painting. Fred brokered a deal with Bruno Bischofberger, the Zurich-based art dealer, where he commissioned a series of portraits of significant 20th Century figures, chosen by Andy. Andy picked Mao Zedong as his first subject. Using the frontispiece of the *Quotations of Chairman Mao*, he produced a huge number of screenprints – around 2000, in a great variety of colours, with Warholian squiggles added. Revolutionary chic was in: once again Andy had struck the right chord, but whilst he admired the power of Mao Zedong's image and was fascinated by the excellence of Chinese propaganda, he didn't feel the same way about Nixon. In a rare political intervention, Andy produced a set of images demonising Nixon for the George McGovern Presidential campaign. When Nixon won by a landslide that November, Andy, together with other Democrat-supporting artists, were placed under an IRS taxation investigation.

WHO?
MAO ZEDONG,
FOUNDING FATHER OF THE PEOPLE'S REPUBLIC OF CHINA,
CHINESE LEADER 1949-76.

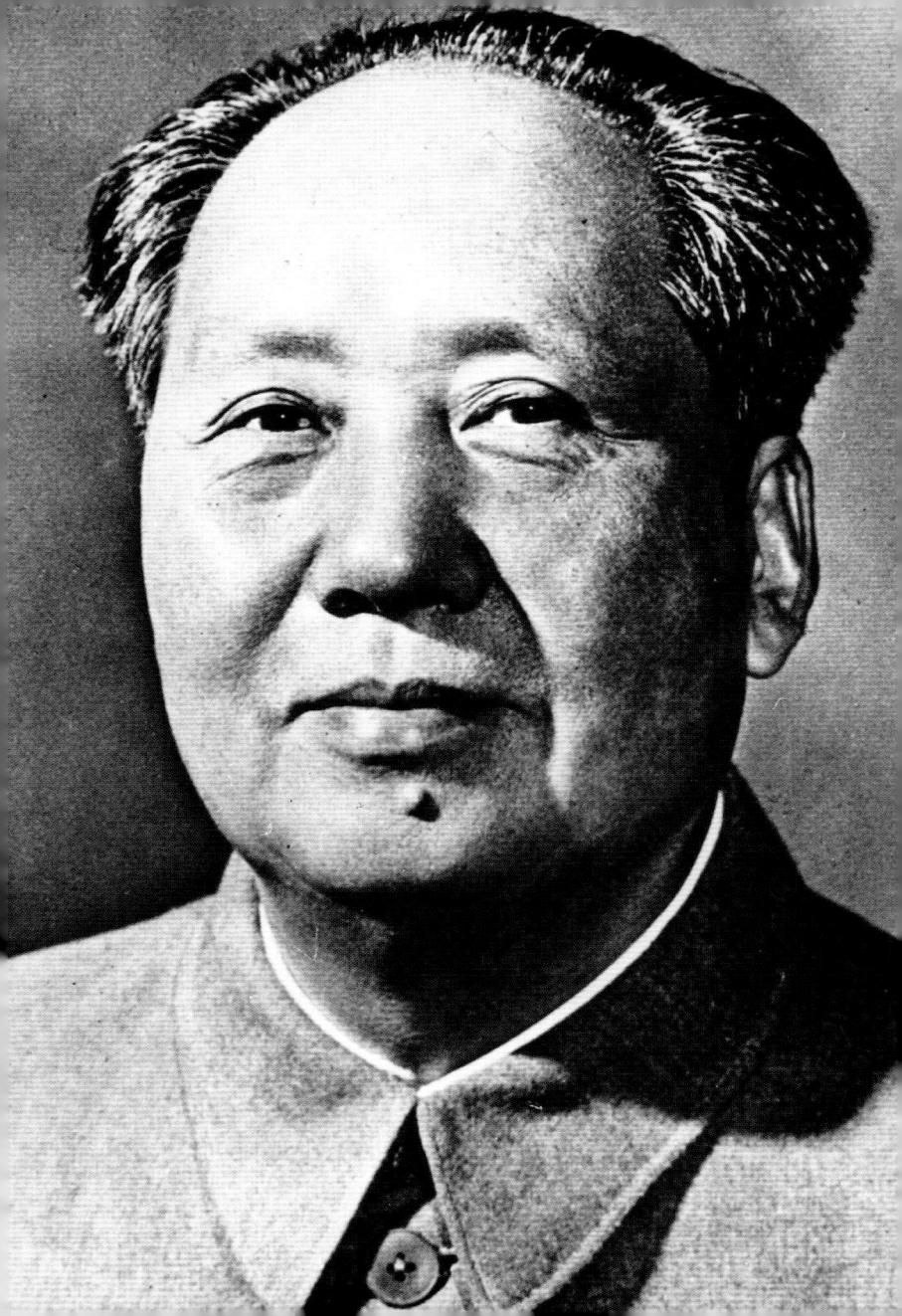

ST MORITZ

"Switzerland is my favourite place now, because it's so nothing, and everybody's rich." Andy Warhol

As his wealth increased, so Andy started to hang out with a glamorous billionaire crowd. He, Fred Hughes and Jed joined the newsprint mogul Peter Brant and his wife Sandy in St Moritz on holiday in winter 1972. Peter Brant was a good friend of Leo Castelli's and already an avid collector. Fred and Andy knew that pleasure would be mixed with new portrait business in St Moritz: the likes of the Agnellis, Niarchoses and Gunter Sachs (heir to the German Opel fortune) were there. They stayed at the Palace Hotel, where Sachs had a long lease on the penthouse, which he had decorated by Lichtenstein, Allen Jones and Yves Klein. Sachs and Warhol became close friends, and Sachs commissioned a portrait of himself and a few of Brigitte Bardot, his then wife. Andy didn't ski, nor did he do the Cresta Run. He spent his whole time hanging in the lobby, doing press interviews (just sitting there staring enigmatically, whilst Fred answered the questions).

WHERE?
THE PALACE HOTEL,
ST MORITZ.

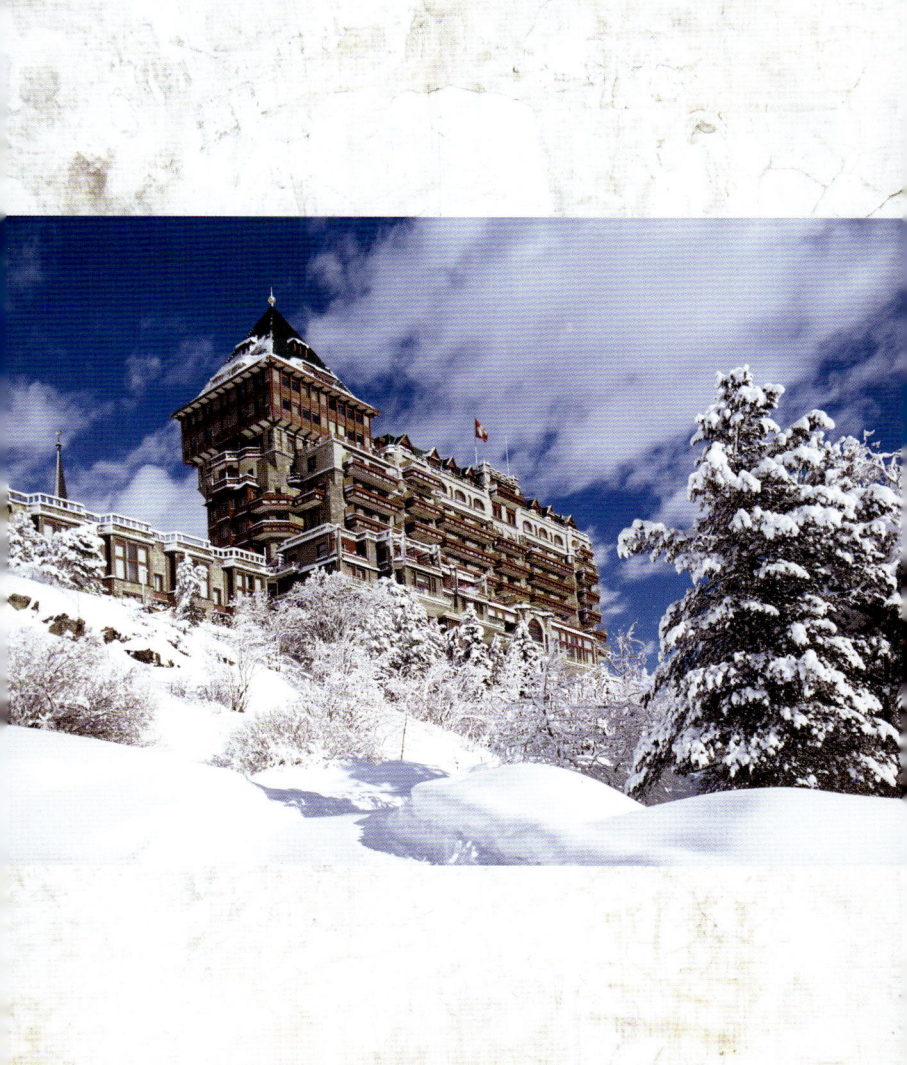

PARIS 2

"Yves Saint Laurent is the most important French artist." Andy Warhol

The Warhol style was also changing. Gone were the t-shirts and leather jackets, in were Savile Row suits and ties. It was Fred, who had worked in the city before the Factory, who got Andy hooked on Paris. They travelled together with the Brants, adding Art Deco pieces to Andy's collection. In 1970 Warhol shot a movie in Karl Lagerfeld's apartment, *L'Amour*, and Fred then bought a flat there. Andy and Fred began to mix with Parisian beau monde: Paloma Picasso, Yves Saint Laurent and his partner Pierre Bergé, and LouLou de la Falaise. Warhol rather loved Paris because the critics loved him – much more so than in New York. Warhol duly created portraits of Yves in 1972 and of his bulldog, Moujik, in 1986.

WHERE?
ANDY AT A PARTY WITH YSL,
PARIS, 1972.

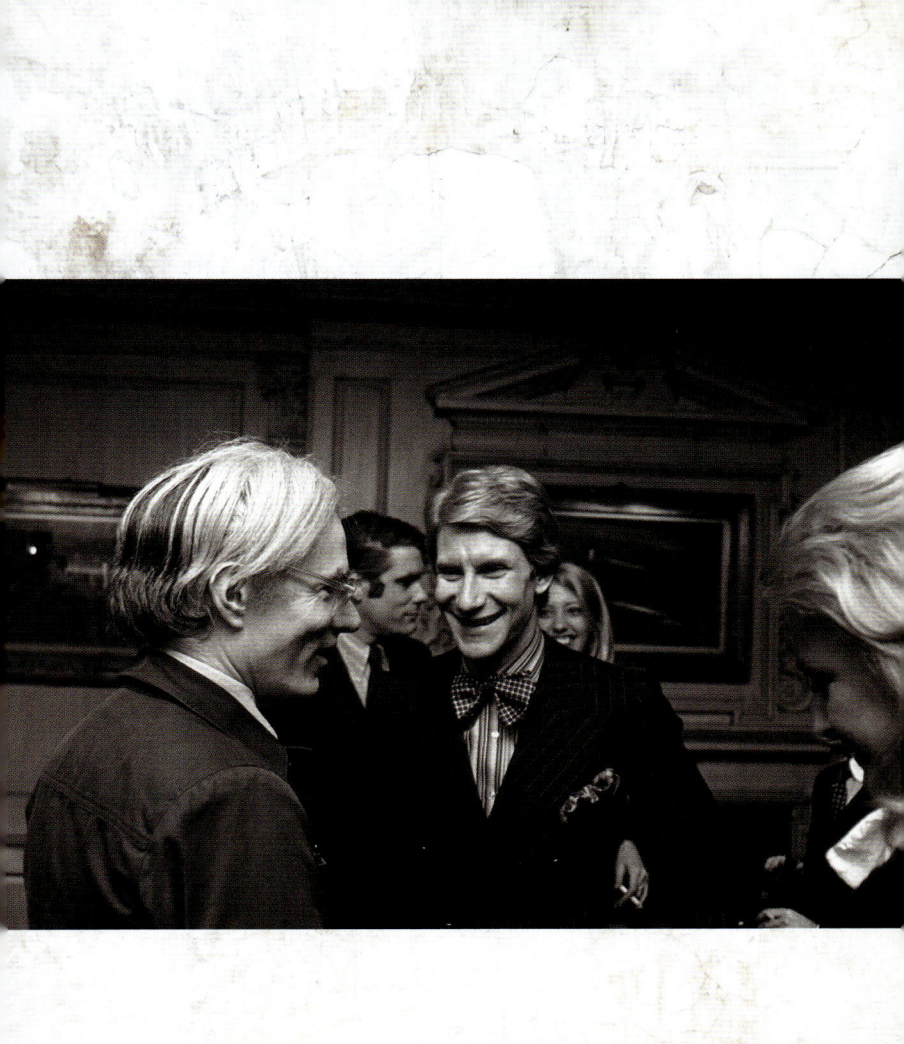

CINECITTÁ

"This is the real Hollywood, Cinecittá... La Dolce Vita, everybody fantastic!"
Andy Warhol

Where Hollywood gave Warhol and his team the cold shoulder, another sign that Europe was much more receptive to the Pope of Pop was Carlo Ponti's enthusiasm for Warhol's movies. Ponti was Sophia Loren's husband and the producer of *La Strada*, *Doctor Zhivago*, *Zabriskie Point* and *Blow Up*. In the summer of 1973 he agreed to bankroll, to the tune of $700,000 ($4.1 million in today's terms), with Polanski as a silent partner, two Warhol movies: *Flesh for Frankenstein* and *Blood for Dracula*. Warhol was pleased to get a fee up front and a generous royalty share of profits. Ponti held onto distribution. Andy loved making a properly financed movie. He jetted back and forth to New York (to do portrait commissions). In Rome he met Elizabeth Taylor. Released in November 1973, *Frankenstein* was a hit, grossing $4million in the USA alone, and over $20 million worldwide. But somehow, Ponti managed not to make a profit. Andy received not a dime in royalties. La Dolce Vita was not so dolce after all.

WHERE?
ENTRANCE TO THE CINECITTÁ FILM STUDIOS,
MUNICIPIO VII,
ROME.

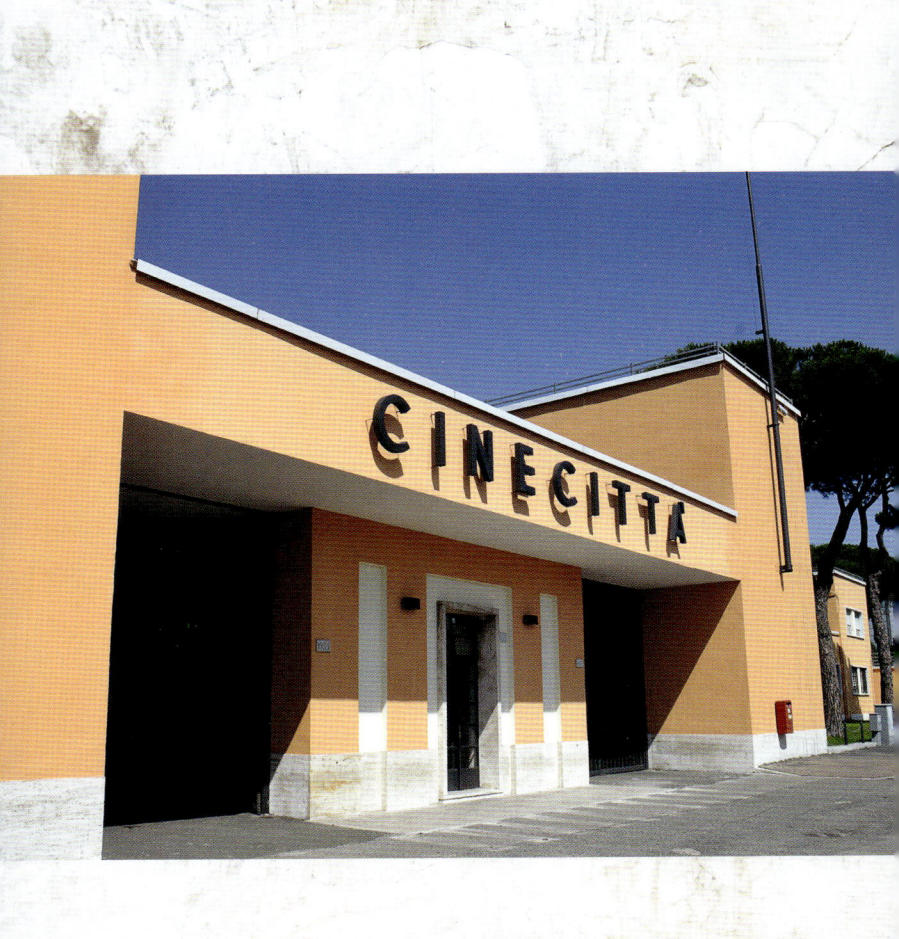

INTERVIEW

"Let's make it a magazine for people like us!" Fred Hughes

Andy had created *Interview* in 1969 on a whim as an underground magazine mostly about movies, mostly so Factory staffers could pose as journalists to get press passes. It lost money year on year, with most of its declared circulation being free copies. Andy thought about closing it. Then, in 1973, Fred Hughes had a brainwave: make it a magazine about celebrities for celebrities. The wannabes would have a shop window into their lives. The advertisers would love it if their merchandise was mentioned. Hughes appointed the clever Bob Colacello as editor. Serious investment was brought in: Bischofberger and Peter Brant. It was witty, edgy, unashamedly fawning towards power, success and conspicuous consumption. Bob had suggested Warhol do a column, but he said "no Bob, you do it." His column, wittily entitled *OUT* (he may have been out and about, but was also so 'in'), described the endless parties, and, always, what 'X' or 'Y' wore. Advertising revenue and circulation shot up. The glamour, of course, all rubbed off on Andy.

WHERE
INTERVIEW PARTY AT STUDIO 54, FOR THE DEBBIE HARRY ISSUE.
FROM LEFT: HENRY GELDZAHLER, LORNA LUFT, JERRY HALL,
ANDY, DEBBIE, TRUMAN CAPOTE, PALOMA PICASSO.

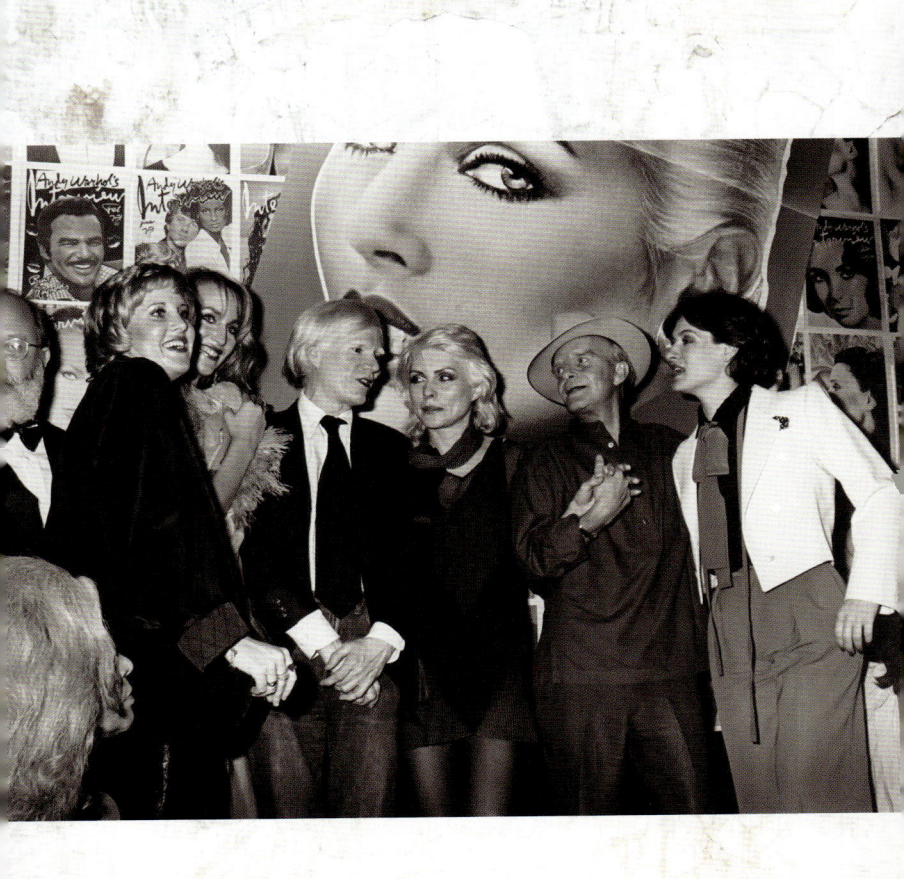

1974–1987

The move to his uber-elegant Upper East Side mansion at first seemed like a fitting symbol for Andy from the mid-70s onwards: the very wealthy, celebrated portrait painter to the stars. He, Fred Hughes and Bob Colacello spent much time courting uber-wealthy dictators, such as the Shah of Iran and Imelda Marcos, despite mounting criticism. Andy had returned to full party mode, particularly at the legendary Studio 54. Another sign that he had reached a pinnacle of renown were his invitations to White House banquets. But his dealers, particularly Bruno Bischofberger, recognised that Andy was losing his edge. He needed to plug in to new directions in art, specifically those artists that had come out of the graffiti scene. The result was a collaboration with the brilliant young black artist, Jean-Michel Basquiat. It wasn't entirely successful, but a show of self-portraits in London in 1986 was. Andy, surprisingly, now turned centuries back for inspiration, producing works inspired by Leonardo's *Last Supper*, completed in 1498. Many of his works were now religiously inspired, an illustration that Andy's Ruthenian Roman Catholicism had never left him. Then in 1987 Andy finally decided to have the routine gall bladder operation that he had resisted for many years. Tragically, this time he would not survive.

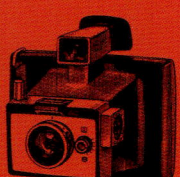

Andy's Polaroids

Andy loved the instant gratification that Polaroid cameras offered. They also provided a very quick way of doing his portraits. He could capture people at candid moments, looking pretty ordinary, transform the image by blowing it up, and then screenprint a hyper-glamourised portrait. The paradox of making iconic images from a throwaway, almost trashy process, which serious photographers sneered at, was not lost on Andy. He knew well that that was what made it fun, ironic, and very 'now.'

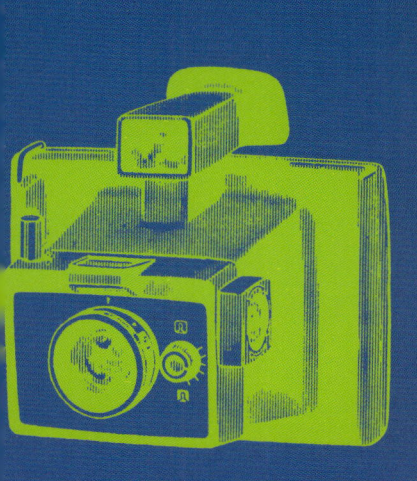
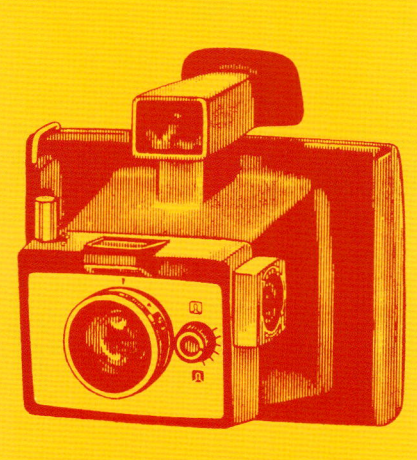
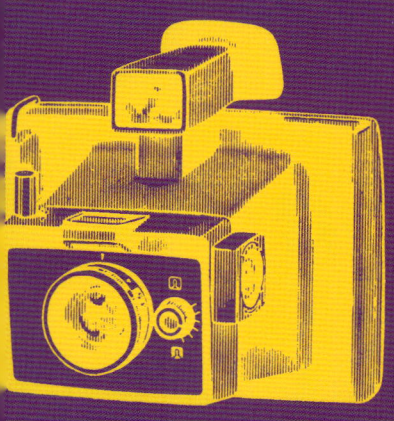
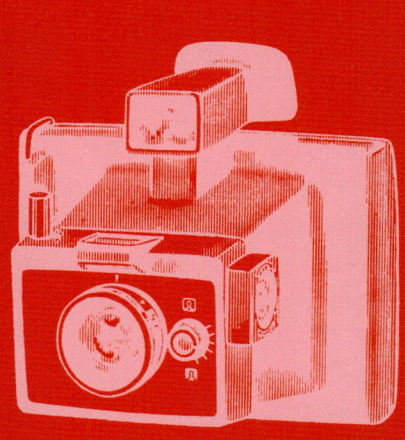

1

FACTORY (NO. 3)

"Pretty much everyone he hired came... from upper-middle class families."
Bob Colacello, on the Broadway Factory.

After the Cinecittà debacle, Andy decided he wanted a change. It was surprising that he had kept Factory 2 on, given the shooting. The new Factory on 860 Broadway was only half a block away and offered more space, not least for *Interview*'s expanding staff. Even though AWE was flush with cash, Andy hilariously insisted that the move be done on foot. Anyone who came by the Factory was asked to carry something to the new location. 'The Office' as it was now called, moved into business gear. Andy would ask Bob constantly how circulation was doing in this or that hick town, or give him ideas for new advertisers. Bob and Fred were already on commission for portraits. Now Andy incentivised the rest of the team (whilst keeping their salaries pitifully modest). A single portrait was $25,000, $15,000 for a second, $10,000 for a third, $5,000 for a fourth. It was a production line. Andy would take polaroids of his subjects, a printer converted them into large proofs, Andy traced onto canvas, added colours, then they were silk-screened. In today's terms, 'The Office' was now turning over $55 million a year.

WHERE?
ANDY IN THE THIRD FACTORY, WITH HIS BELOVED ARCHIE, AT 860 BROADWAY, MANHATTAN.

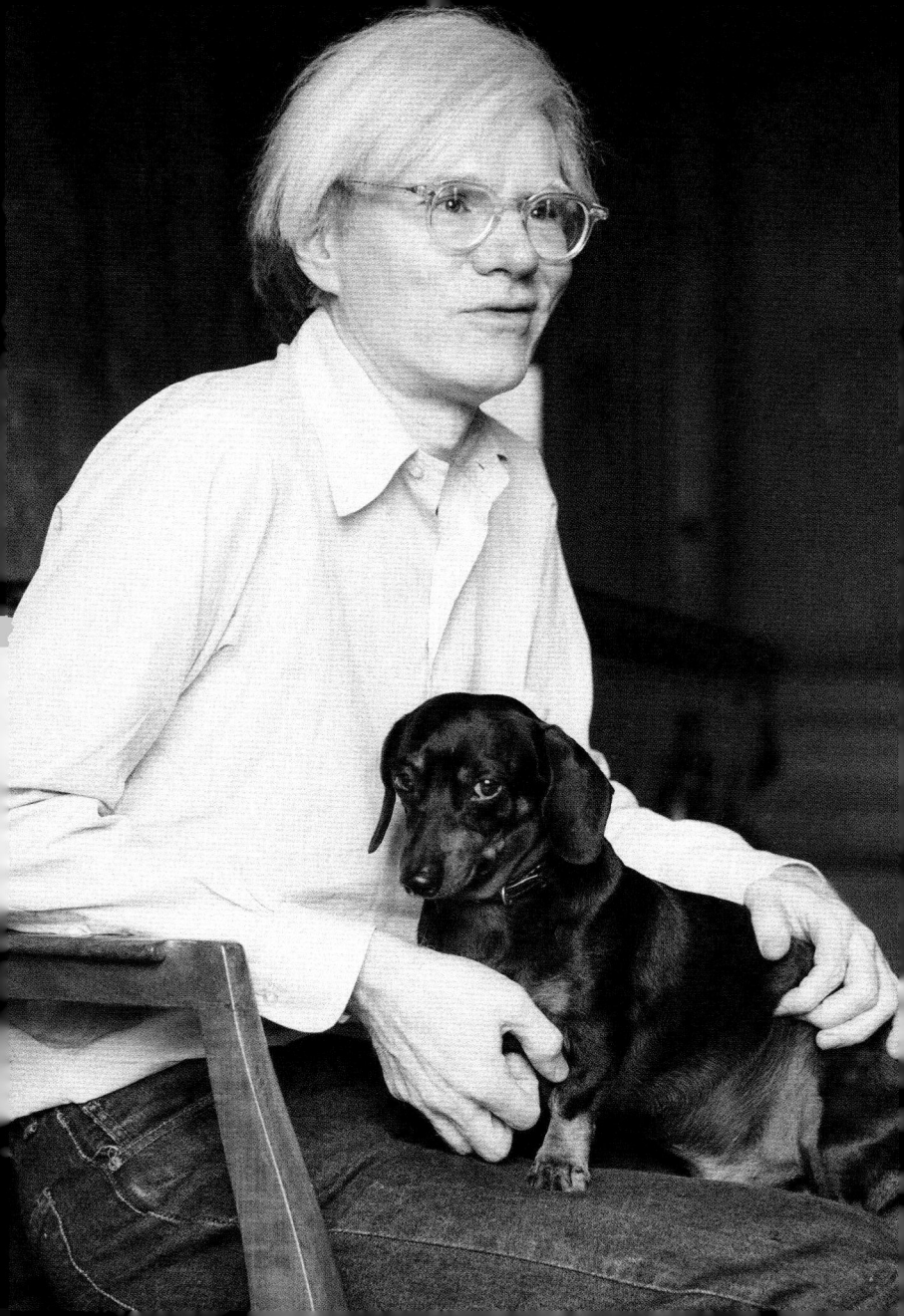

6

THE HALSTON HOUSE

"Halston and Warhol both had a sophisticated appreciation for the power of brand identity." **Nicholas Chambers**

Andy and Halston, the uber-fashionable clothes designer of simple, relaxed US chic, had much in common. They were both from out of town – Warhol from Pittsburgh and Halston from Des Moines, Iowa – both had rising success in the '60s consolidated in the '70s, both were gay and both had been window-dressers. They were aware of each others' work before they became friends. Halston had commissioned a portrait from Andy and hung Warhol prints in his stunning party house by architect Paul Rudolph. It was Halston's boyfriend Victor Hugo who helped cement the friendship between them and by the mid '70s Halston and Andy became inseparable friends, the undisputed leaders of the Manhattan social scene. Andy hung out frequently at parties, with Liza Minnelli and Bianca Jagger, at the Halston House, before they would go and hold court at the latest 'in' club. Andy took to wearing Halston, and Halston created scarf and dress designs inspired by Andy's flower prints. Lovers, no, but best friends, undoubtedly yes.

WHERE?
101 EAST 63RD STREET, MANHATTAN.
RECENTLY ON THE MARKET FOR $28 MILLION.

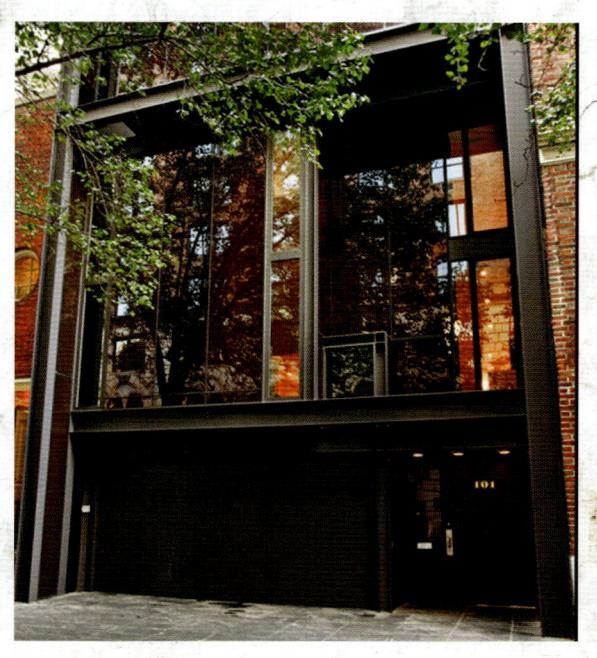

ANDY'S 1974 WORLD TOUR

As Andy Warhol Enterprises got into gear, Andy accepted that, in the interests of business (society portraits), international travel was part of the deal. His three week global tour in October 1974 would set a pattern. It was usually New York/ Paris/ Milan/ Tokyo and sometimes London, with refuelling stops on the way. Fred and Bob ensured that as many celebrities as possible would be on hand at each destination, so that the all-important portrait commissions would roll in.

⑤ ANCHORAGE

A refuelling stop on the way to Tokyo. Andy endured the 24 hour flight with cassettes, mostly of operas, and reading celebrity biographies.

❶ NEW YORK

Andy left New York with his usual entourage of Fred Hughes, Bob Colacello (who would write the trip up in his OUT column in *Interview*) and boyfriend Jed Johnson.

❷ PARIS

In Paris they stayed at the George V. Andy was photographed, jet-lagged, by Helmut Newton. They had dinner with Eric de Rothschild (hoping for a portrait commission), went to parties and nightclubs and Andy met up with David Hockney.

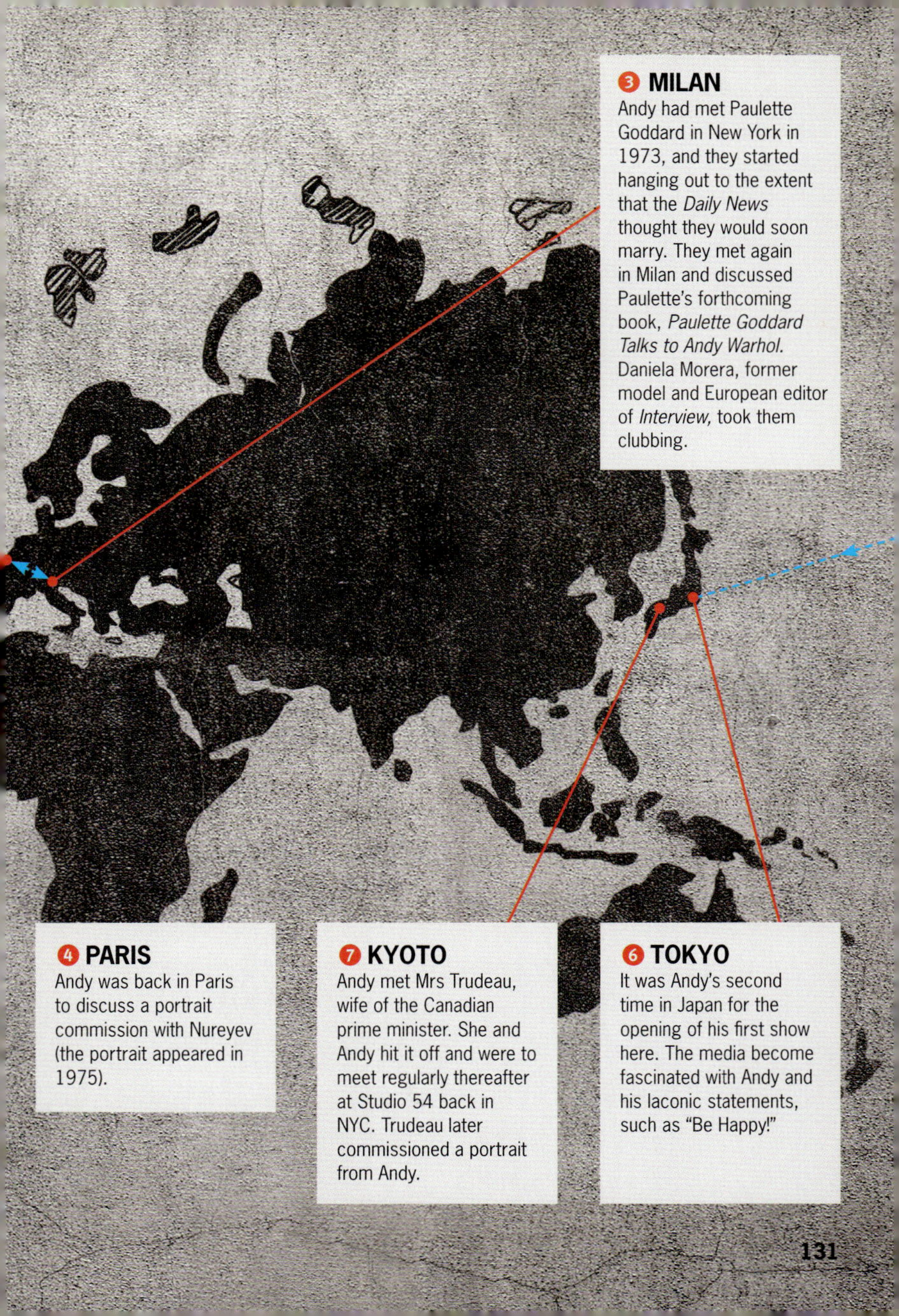

Andy had met Paulette Goddard in New York in 1973, and they started hanging out to the extent that the *Daily News* thought they would soon marry. They met again in Milan and discussed Paulette's forthcoming book, *Paulette Goddard Talks to Andy Warhol*. Daniela Morera, former model and European editor of *Interview*, took them clubbing.

❹ **PARIS**

Andy was back in Paris to discuss a portrait commission with Nureyev (the portrait appeared in 1975).

❼ **KYOTO**

Andy met Mrs Trudeau, wife of the Canadian prime minister. She and Andy hit it off and were to meet regularly thereafter at Studio 54 back in NYC. Trudeau later commissioned a portrait from Andy.

❻ **TOKYO**

It was Andy's second time in Japan for the opening of his first show here. The media become fascinated with Andy and his laconic statements, such as "Be Happy!"

2

57 EAST 66TH STREET

"It's got the traditional old money look I'm after." Andy Warhol

As well as moving the Factory, Andy decided on a new house; Julia's death may have precipitated the decision. As usual he got a great deal – he paid around $2.5 million in today's prices, for this 8,000 square foot Upper East Side mansion (it was on the market for $35 million in 2008). Andy didn't sell Lexington Avenue – he rented it to Fred. At East 66th Street, Jed took charge of the redecorations, with instructions to keep cornices, fireplaces and other period details intact. The house had vast entertaining spaces, but Andy rarely had anyone over. An early dinner party with Diana Vreeland and Truman Capote was just embarrassing, he said. Other than Andy, it was just Jed and two almost invisible Filipino maids. The house became a mausoleum for Andy's collecting habit. The entire dining room was covered with neat shopping bags with whatever *objet* Andy had bought that morning, wrapped, unopened and dated. Andy preferred to eat in the downstairs kitchen.

WHERE?
ANDY'S HOUSE AT 57 EAST 66TH STREET, MANHATTAN.

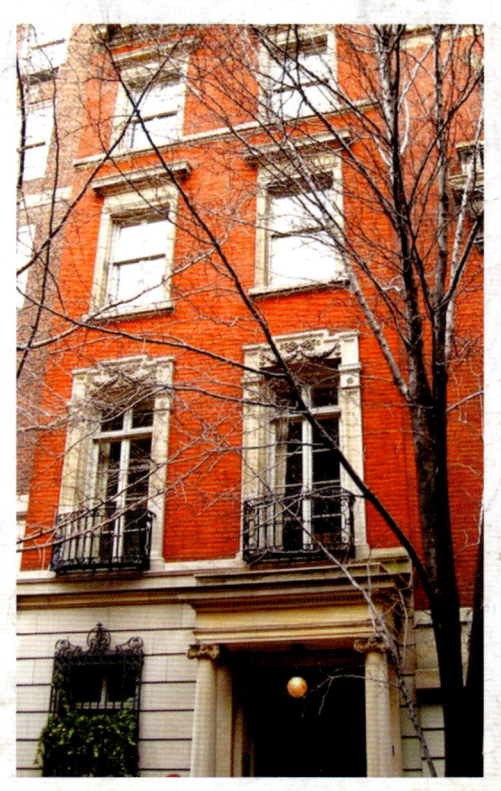

WHAT WAS IN ANDY'S HOUSE?

ENTRANCE HALL:
VERY BIG BUST OF NAPOLEON. SMALLER BUSTS OF LAFAYETTE AND
BENJAMIN FRANKLIN. CHIPPENDALE SOFA. GEORGIAN ARMCHAIR (C. 1720).
AMERICAN ANCESTRAL PORTRAITS. FULL–SIZE MALE NUDE, BY GEORGE
BELLOWS, 1906.

DINING ROOM:
FULL-SIZE DINING TABLE, FEDERAL PERIOD, POSSIBLY BY DUNCAN PHYFE, C.
1800. SET OF 12 ART DECO DINNING CHAIRS. AUBUSSON CARPET. AMERICAN
PRIMITIVE PAINTINGS. WOODCUT BY EDVARD MUNCH. ON THE FLOOR:
ENDLESS SHOPPING BAGS, WALL-TO-WALL, OF ANDY'S DAILY PURCHASES,
ALL STILL WRAPPED.

UP ONE FLIGHT OF STAIRS:
LANDING: WOODEN FIGURE OF PUNCH.
FORMAL SITTING ROOM: ARTWORKS AND PAINTINGS BY MODERN AMERICAN
MASTERS: CY TWOMBLY, JAMES ROSENQUIST, CLAES OLDENBURG, ROY
LICHTENSTEIN, JASPER JOHNS.

REAR PARLOUR:
AMERICAN AND FRENCH 18TH AND 19TH SCHOOL PAINTINGS. EMPIRE-STYLE
FURNITURE (C. 1820) IN MARBLE, MAHOGANY AND ORMOLU. URNS AND
CANDELABRAE. NEO-EGYPTIAN FIGURINES. A SECOND BUST OF NAPOLEON.

ANDY'S UPSTAIRS BEDROOM:
MEXICAN CRUCIFIX. MAXFIELD PARRISH PAINTING. FEDERAL PERIOD 4-POSTER
BED. TV SET. STACKED GREEN BOXES HOUSING WIGS.
HIDDEN INSIDE THE BED CANOPY: RINGS, BROOCHES, JEWELS.

GUEST BEDROOM:
SMALL PAINTING OF CHAIRMAN MAO
(THE ONLY WARHOL IN THE HOUSE, IN A ROOM RARELY USED).

OTHER UPSTAIRS ROOMS:
ANDY'S 610 CARDBOARD 'TIME CAPSULES'.

ANDY'S BATHROOM CABINET, OVER 100 JARS INCLUDING:
XERAC ACNE CREAM. EXSEL SELENIUM SCALP LOTION. NOXZEMA SKIN
CLEANSER. LINDA SILVER COLLAGEN CREAM. GSL ANTI-AGEING CREAM.
GLYCEL CELLULAR CLEANSER. HALSTON FOR MEN. GREY FLANNEL BY
GEOFFREY BEENE. HABIT ROUGE BY GUERLAIN. VARIOUS SHELLY MARKS POT
POURRIS.

IN THE GARAGE:
1978 BROWN ROLLS ROYCE SILVER SHADOW.

SQUIRRELLED AWAY IN DRAWERS AND CUPBOARDS EVERYWHERE:
LOTS OF KITSCH JUNK, FROM COKE BOTTLE FIGURINES AND ROCKING
HORSES TO SETS OF BAKELITE PLATES AND 175, 1950S ERA, COOKIE JARS.

THE SOTHEBY'S SALE:
IN 1988, AFTER ANDY'S DEATH, SOTHEBY'S SOLD OFF THE CONTENTS
OF ANDY'S HOUSE, FOR $25.3 MILLION (OVER $55 MILLION AT CURRENT
VALUES). 78 OF THE 175 COOKIE JARS SOLD FOR $250,000 ($517,500
TODAY).

3

CHADDS FORD: WYETHS

"I love his work. I always wished I could paint like him." **Andy on Jamie Wyeth**

Andy travelled seamlessly through various worlds: one minute in Tehran in ultimate luxury with a dictatorial monarchy, the next taking close-up polaroids of gay orgies in some seedy dive, then deciding on a collaboration with the most traditional of US art dynasties. Jamie Wyeth was the artist son of Andrew Wyeth, arguably America's most famous painter. They arranged to paint portraits of each other for a show at the Coe Kerr Gallery. Jamie's portrait showed Warhol, bad skin condition and all, with Archie the dachshund. Warhol's portrait made Jamie look like a Byronesque movie star. The show was a critical success and re-cemented Andy's place in the New York art world. Andy and Jamie became friends, with Andy going down to the Wyeth's idyllic compound at Chadds Ford, Pennsylvania. He didn't soak up the bucolic atmosphere however, spending his time watching soaps on TV. When Andy met Jamie's dad, the great, respectable Andrew Wyeth, they got on surprisingly well.

WHERE?
ANDREW WYETH'S STUDIO,
CHADDS FORD.

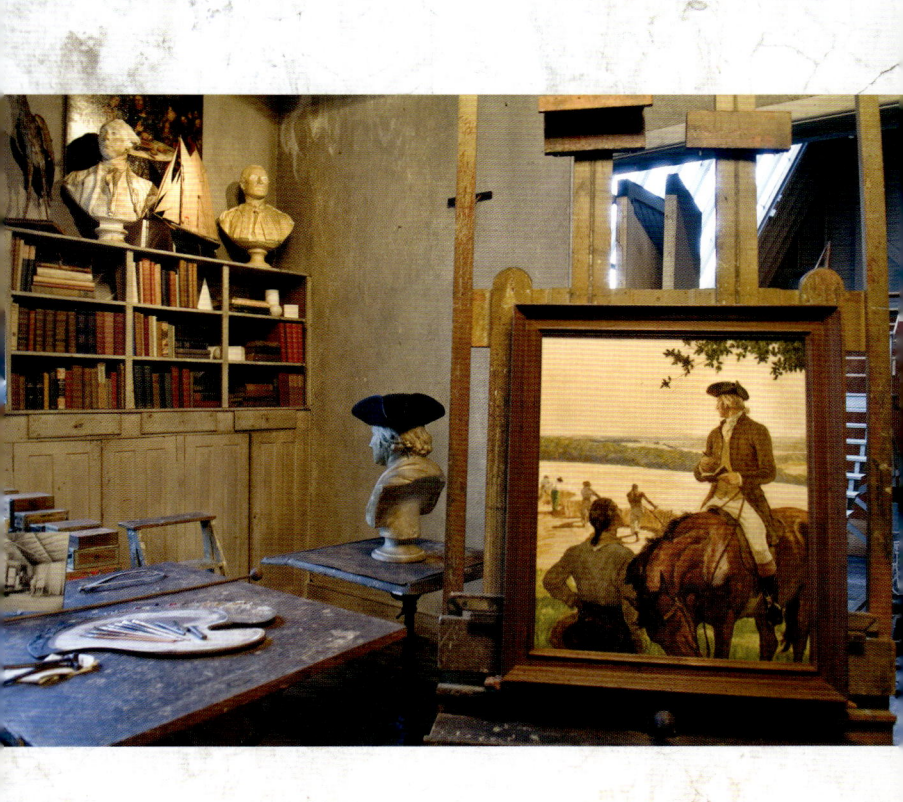

④

TEHRAN

"He loved the fact we could call room service...and get caviar all day long for $10 an order." **Bob Colacello, The Atlantic**

Real money attracted Andy like a moth to a flame, and no one had more than the Shah of Iran and his Pahlavi family. Tehran's ambassador to the UN, Fereydoon Hoveyda, was a great art enthusiast and held a kind of salon at the Iranian consulate in New York, to which Andy was invited. He was taking orders from Empress Farah Pahlavi, who wished to create an amazing contemporary art museum in Tehran. Andy flew out with Bob Colacello and Fred when, to his secret delight, he was at last invited to create a portrait of the Empress. The Tehran they saw, according to Colacello, was mostly like Mulholland Drive in L.A. – chic, ultra-modern villas, swimming pools and western dress. Back home the press, especially *Village Voice*, was sharply critical of the trip – how could Andy suck up to a police state that sanctioned the regular use of medieval-style torture? Andy didn't care. He was astounded by the endless caviar and the peacock throne (50,000 carats of gemstones), and the trip was a big success – 12 portraits for a fee, in today's values, of $860,000, with the prospect of more portraits to follow.

WHERE?
ANDY IN ISFAHAN, IRAN.

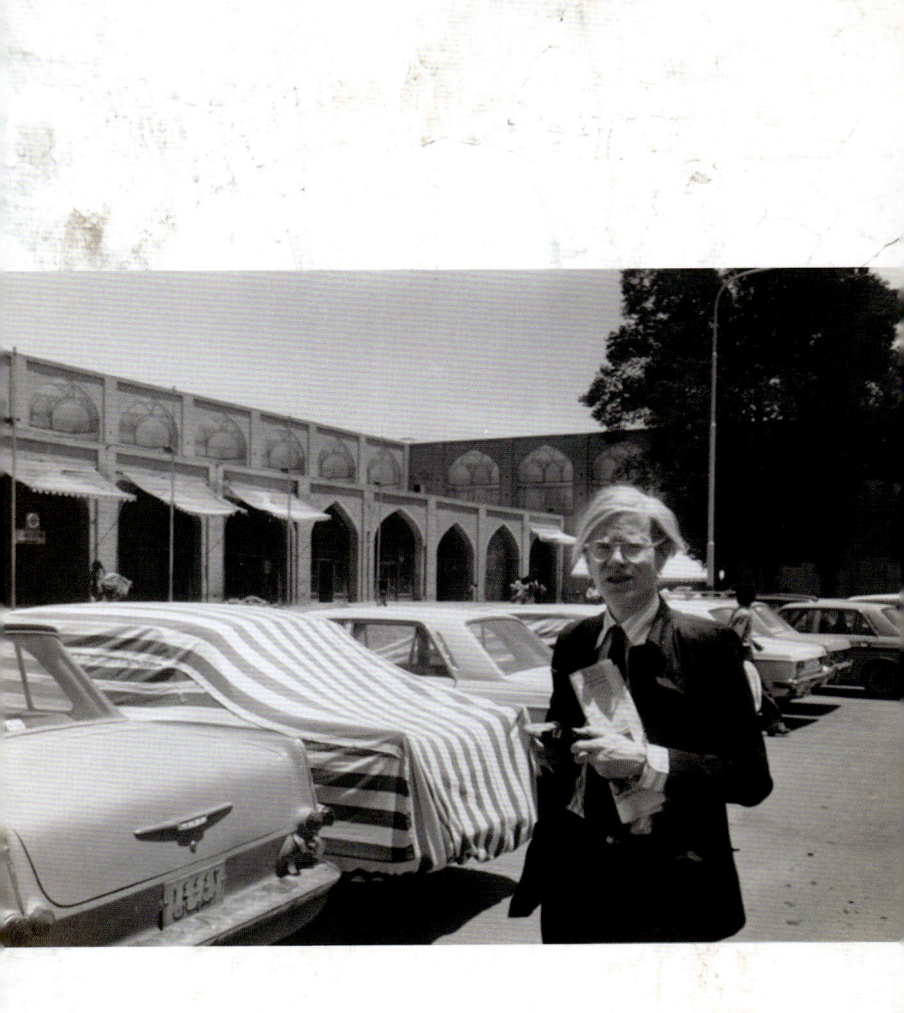

5

STUDIO 54

"Some people say California is the bell-wether of America. I'd say Andy Warhol."
Barbara Goldsmith, New York Times

By 1977, Andy was back in full party mode. *Interview* had redefined luxe decadence. Everyone wanted to be in it. The portrait business was going well. Money was pouring in. New York was on the up. Celebrity excess was in, and nothing captured the mood more than Steve Rubell's and Ian Schrager's glitzy new club, Studio 54.The party was fuelled by healthy doses of cocaine (Andy didn't partake), and the constant presence of the cool, rich and famous. It was almost impossible to get in, ensuring that there were queues of wannabes outside every night. Warhol loved it and became a regular, along with Halston, Bianca Jagger (who turned up on a white stallion for her 30th birthday), Jerry Hall, Mick Jagger, Lisa Minnelli, Liz Taylor, Lorna Luft, Richard Gere, Mariel Hemingway, Jack Nicholson, Grace Jones, Cher, David Bowie, Paloma Picasso, Debbie Harry, Jackie O. and Margaret Trudeau. The party lasted until 1980, when Rubell and Schrager were busted by the IRS: Rubell had said in the *New York Times* that "only the Mafia made more money." He and Shrager were discovered to have skimmed $2.5 million.

WHERE?
BIANCA, ANDY, JERRY HALL AND LORNA LUFT AT STUDIO 54.

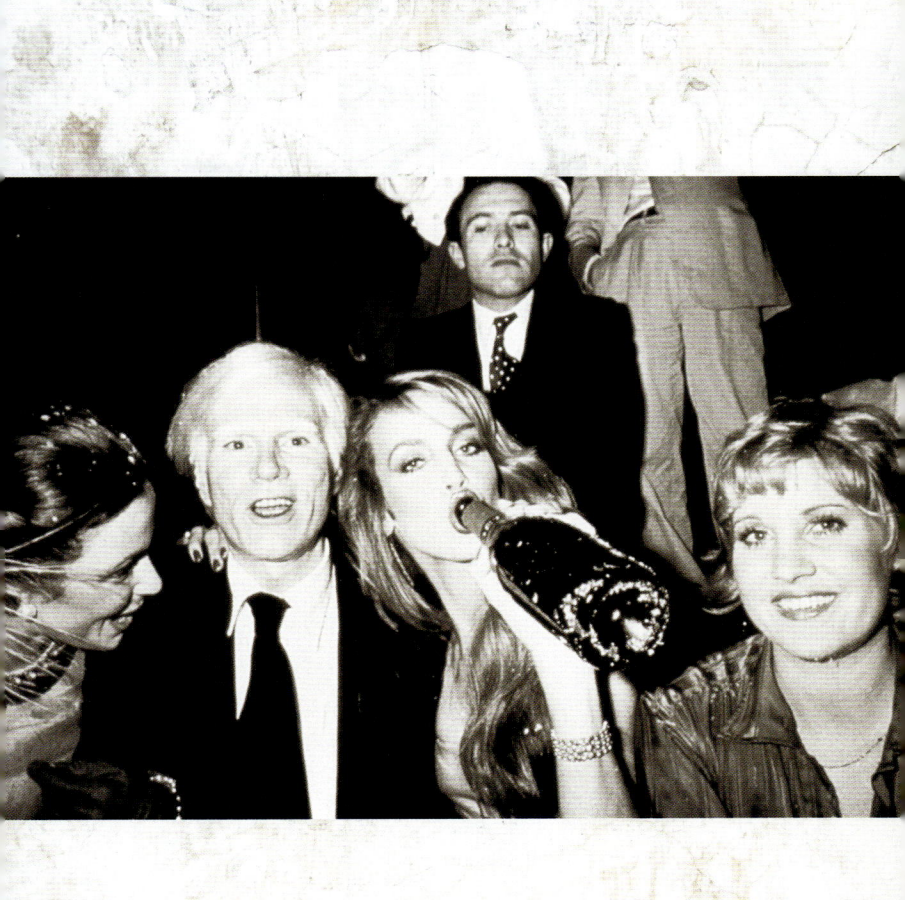

6

THE WHITE HOUSE

"'The White House called'...is really the most glamorous message you can get in the world." Andy Warhol

Andy just loved the White House. His first invitation had come in 1975, thanks to Bianca's connection with Jack Ford, President Gerald Ford's son. Andy and Bob Colacello interviewed him for *Interview*; Betty Ford was outraged. Once Jimmy Carter became president, Andy was invited back to a party for the artists who had supported Carter's election. Back in Manhattan Andy, Fred Hughes and Bob Colacello were getting closer to the Pahlavi regime, attending regular events at the Iranian embassy. Despite being a Democrat, Andy was fascinated by power and wealth and did not feel he had to square the contradiction. So he was thrilled again when an invitation came to a state dinner at the White House from Carter for the Shah and Empress of Iran in November 1977 (the US had agreed export deals for its companies worth $50 billion). Sadly for Andy, the party was about to end: 14 months following the visit the Shah was deposed, and Iran became a strict, repressive, theocratic Islamic republic.

WHERE?
ANDY AT A STATE BANQUET
FOR THE SHAH OF IRAN AT THE WHITE HOUSE.

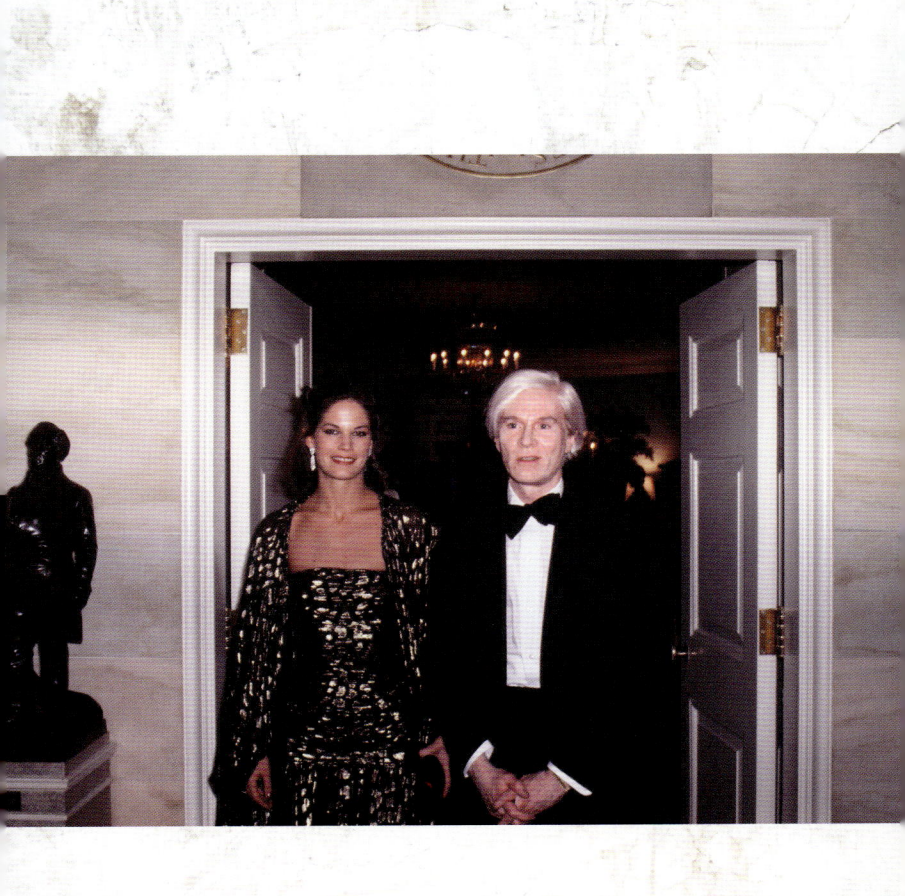

7

THE MUDD CLUB

"I would go to the opening of anything... including a toilet seat."
Andy Warhol

Andy was thought of as an icon by the punk and new wave scene which was emerging in mid-to-late '70s Manhattan. Blondie, the Talking Heads and The Clash all turned up at the Factory. Andy understood that in order to feed his edginess, he had to be across what was new. In 1978 that meant the Mudd Club, newly opened down in then ungentrified Tribeca, as a deliberate downtown antidote to the glitz of uptown Studio 54. Mudd was where Blondie, Nico, The Cramps, The B-52s and David Byrne hung out. Keith Haring curated a gallery on the fourth floor. Basquiat and his band Gray played there. Ginsberg and Burroughs gave readings. Andy would turn up regularly – he knew the first silver Factory had been an inspiration for Mudd's founder, Steve Mass. Appearing at the Mudd kept feeding Warhol's image as the continuing oracle of cool. In Warhol's wake, Bowie, Mick Jagger and Grace Jones also became regulars. After a while, inevitably, it lost its edge, closing in 1983.

WHERE?
JEAN-MICHEL BASQUIAT PLAYING WITH GRAY AT
THE MUDD CLUB, 1978.

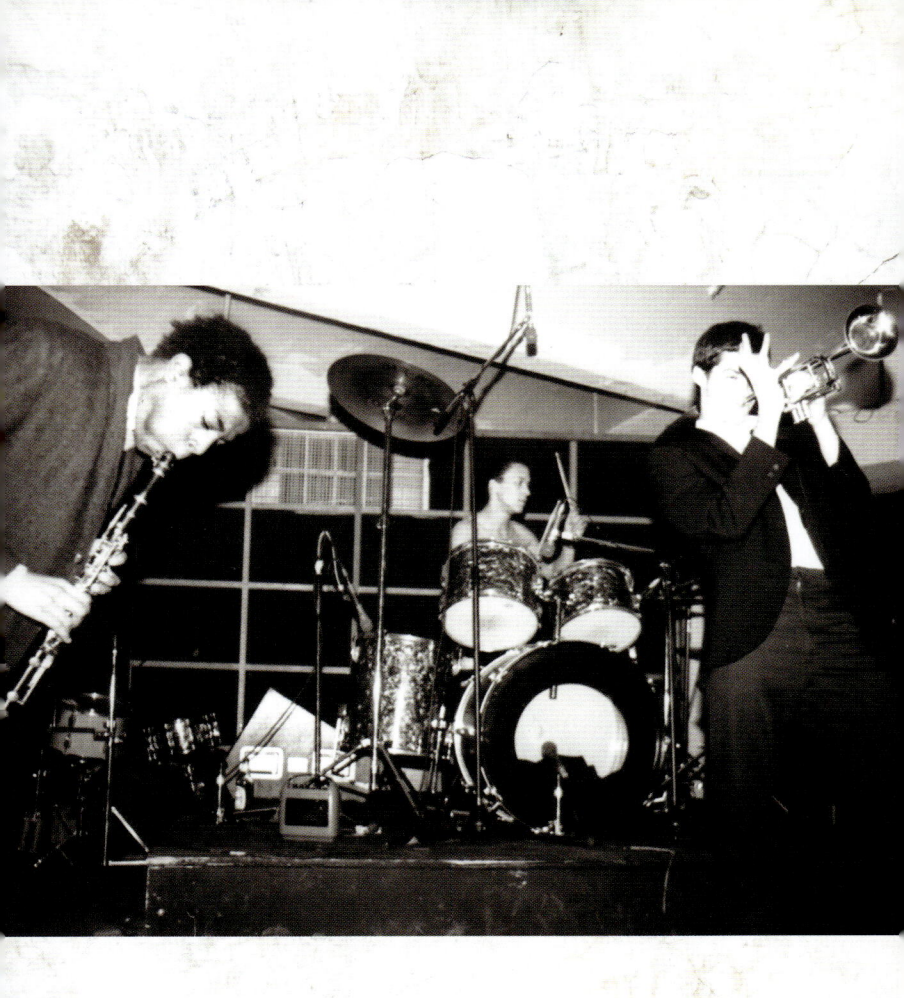

8

ANDY WARHOL TV

"Warhol coveted TV stardom."
The Daily Telegraph

Andy had conquered commercial art and the high-end global art market. He had produced movies, written books, created *Interview* and started a publishing company, Andy Warhol Books. TV was the next frontier. Andy loved trash TV. Back in 1969 he had created a format for his own TV show – *Nothing Special*. A reality TV idea, of people arguing, based on *Chelsea Girls* followed. Neither saw the light of day. In 1978 Andy pitched to NBC the *Nothing Special* idea, got the promise of $375,000 (in today's values) seed funding, but then got cold feet and pulled out as he wouldn't have complete control. Manhattan Cable was the answer. *Andy Warhol's TV*, a televisual companion to *Interview*, was way before its time. A typical episode might involve Bianca Jagger interviewing Spielberg on a hotel bed, with Warhol perched on the end pitching in with his dead-pan observations: "The people in your movies are so real...but good looking too, which is nice." The banal, anti-intellectual Warholian line in questioning made vacuous, but compulsive, viewing. The show ran for 27 episodes, before morphing in 1985 into an MTV show, *Andy Warhol's Fifteen Minutes*. Andy was, at last, on national TV.

WHAT?
ANDY BEING INTERVIEWED ON TV, C.1978.

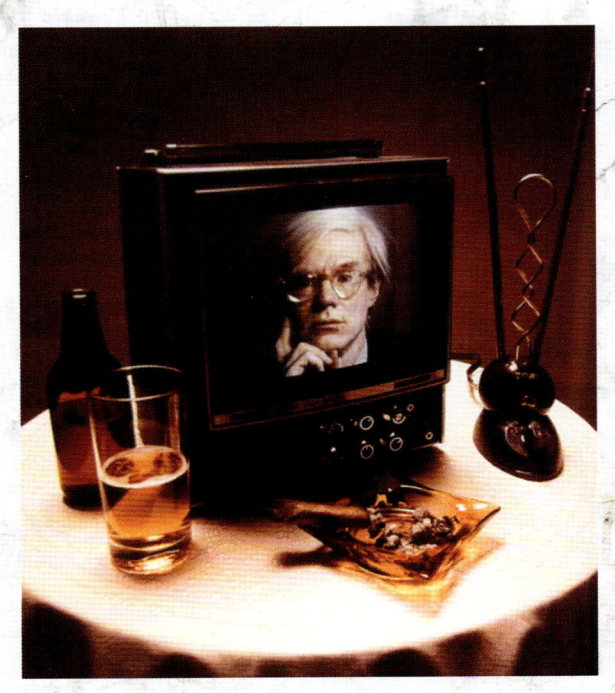

TWO WEEKS IN THE LIFE

FRIDAY JULY 23RD 1982
Andy flies to Montauk by seaplane with Halston. They meet with Bianca Jagger.

SATURDAY JULY 24TH
Hangs in Montauk with Ian Schrager and Steve Rubell (founders of Studio 54), reading books, watching TV and 'talking intellectual.'
Dines with Victor, Schrager and Rubell.

SUNDAY JULY 25TH
Hangs in Montauk, flies back to Manhattan in the afternoon.

MONDAY JULY 26TH
Works in The Factory. Goes and models at a show at Studio 54 at 9.30pm.
Goes to a party at Heartbreak Discotheque.

TUESDAY JULY 27TH
Works in the Factory. Goes to Madison Square Garden to see a Billy Squier and Queen concert. Goes to new discotheque, The Palace, on 14th Street.

WEDNESDAY JULY 28TH
Works at the Factory.
Gets invited out to Fire Island by Calvin Klein for the weekend. Buys a set of giant aluminium set of teeth, to add to the kitsch at home.

THURSDAY JULY 29TH
Works at the Factory.
Drops in at Suzie Frankfurt's. Goes to Serendipity. Goes to Xenon nightclub. Howard Stein and Cornelia Guest are there and she invites Andy to a party in East Hampton at the weekend.

FRIDAY JULY 30TH
Works at the Factory.

148

SATURDAY JULY 31ST
Flies to Fire Island. Stays with Calvin Klein and hangs out with David Geffen, Chester Weinberg, Ian Shrager and Steve Rubell. Goes to a Hawaiin party at Gil de la Cruz's. Goes back to Calvin Klein's and walks in on Calvin, Steve and two porn stars, Knoll and Ford. Forgoes the 4 am Fire Island gay cruise.

SUNDAY AUGUST 1ST
Has brunch at Gil de la Cruz's with Diane Von Furstenberg. Flies back by seaplane to Manhattan. Pilot offers Andy cocaine. Says 'no'.

MONDAY AUGUST 2ND
Works at the Factory. Is visited by Indira Gandhi's daughter-in-law, when he was expecting the daughter (i.e. prospect for a portrait commission).
Goes to Michaele Volbracht's lunch party. Goes to Diane Von Furstenberg's cosmetics launch party.

TUESDAY AUGUST 3RD
Works at the Factory.

WEDNESDAY AUGUST 4TH
Works at the Factory.

THURSDAY AUGUST 5TH
Watches *Tarzan* on cable TV in the morning. Works at the Factory. Shouts at everybody. Introduces aspiring artist Robyn to Alexandre Iolas (Iolas had discovered Warhol in 1952).

FRIDAY AUGUST 6TH
Andy's birthday. Wanders around his neighbourhood looking to find someone to have coffee with. Goes to publicity shoot for Dustin Hoffman's *Tootsie*, then discovers he's in the movie. Works at the Factory. Goes for a stroll up Central Park West. Calls Linda Stein. She invites him to her party for Elton John (following his first night concert at Madison Square Garden). Hangs out there with Timothy Hutton (*Ordinary People*) and Jennifer Grey (*Dirty Dancing*).

9

ST VINCENT FERRER

"...a side to [his] character that he hid from all but his closest friends: his spiritual side." **John Richardson**

Andy never spoke about his Ruthenian Catholic faith, but it was deeply embedded from childhood. He regularly attended this Catholic church on Lexington Avenue, popping in between services every Sunday, sometimes attending mass, but very rarely taking communion and leaving before the sign of peace. Towards the end of his life Andy created images based on his faith, of Leonardo's *Last Supper* (which had hung in the Warholas' kitchen in Pittsburgh), of thrift store images of Christ (treated as a consumer object) and of repeated images of the cross. Many have drawn similarities between the repetition in Catholic liturgy and Warhol's imagery; Jeanette Winterson observed: "The rosary is repetition, the liturgy is repetition, the iconography of the Catholic Church depends on repetition." As to squaring his faith and the drugs, overt straight and gay sex (the Church disapproved), Factory suicides... that was between Andy and his maker. Did he go to confession? Or was Andy just an innocent artist, holding up a mirror to US society?

WHERE?
CATHOLIC CHURCH OF ST. VINCENT FERRER,
869 LEXINGTON AVENUE, MANHATTAN.

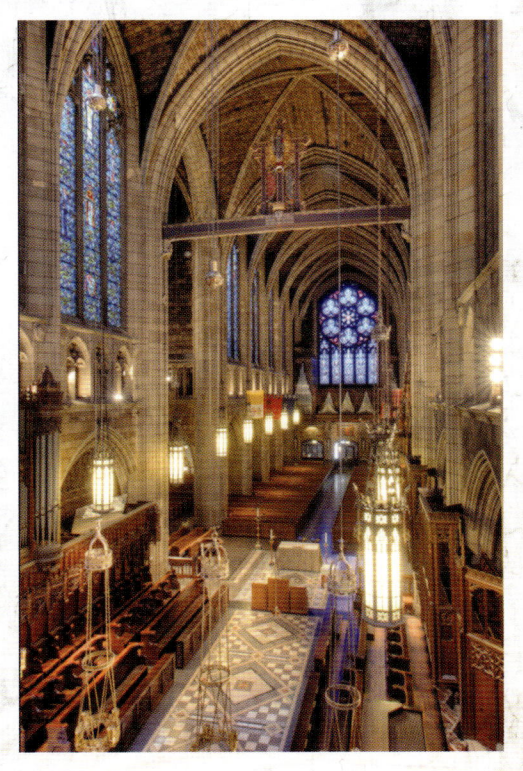

10

THE ANVIL

"The spectators themselves were the performers." Neil Miller

In the late '70s Andy became particularly fascinated with the hardcore BDSM gay scene in New York. Andy loved to go and watch the fisting shows, golden showers, whipping, bondage and anonymous fucking at gay clubs that were then emerging in Manhattan, such as the Mineshaft, the Toilet, and his favourite, the Anvil. The inside of the Anvil was painted black, with a dance area and bar on the ground floor. In the basement was another bar, with non-stop gay porn projected onto a screen. Behind the screen was the performance area. Robert Mapplethorpe, also Catholic, and whom Andy dismissed as "..dirty; his feet smell; he has no money," also became fascinated by the scene, both as participant and photographer. He worshipped Warhol, but Warhol wasn't interested. Once Mapplethorpe had made it, Andy of course relented, and they exchanged portraits. When Mapplethorpe contracted HIV/AIDS, Andy, with the ignorance typical of the time, refused to see him, because he was "diseased." The Anvil was closed in 1986 by the City of New York, at the height of the AIDS scare.

WHERE?
THE ANVIL, 500 WEST 14TH STREET,
MANHATTAN.

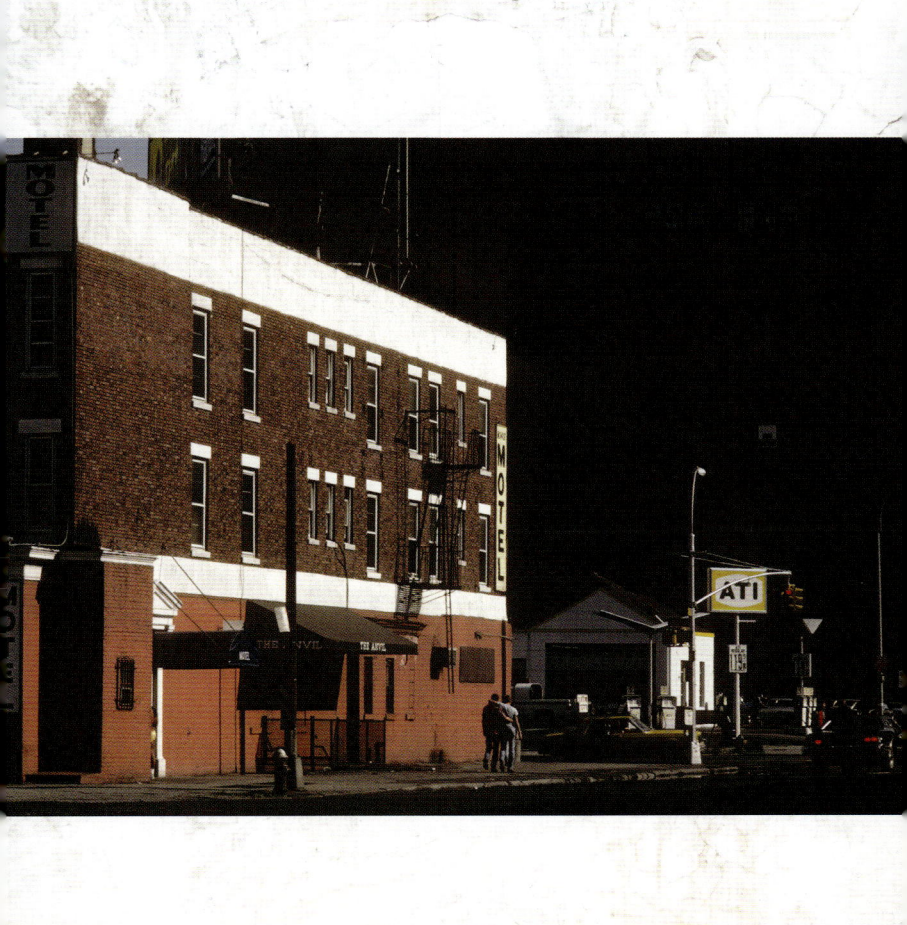

11

THE FACTORY (NO. 4)

"Art is an investment. You can't just love it. You have to love it if it goes up."
Andy Warhol

The money may have been rolling in, but it was clear to the critics
that the art was suffering. In 1980 Andy was producing boilerplate
commissions, such as *Ten Portraits of Jews of the Twentieth Century*
(each set of paintings and prints selling for $875,000 in today's terms),
a set of US mythical heroes (Mickey Mouse, Uncle Sam, Superman) and
a commission from *Playboy* of US athletes. In tandem, a show of his
dollar paintings at Castelli's in 1982 sold not a single work. Andy was
irritated but undaunted. He now decided it was time for another move,
to this stunning, five storey former Con Edison generator station. Andy
bought the whole building and invested $3 million on its conversion. He
at last had a ballroom-sized space in which to paint (on the third floor),
and there was room to store hundreds of his vast canvases. Gratifyingly
his early work was now worth more than ever; two of his works
Saturday Popeye and *Dick Tracy* sold for over $1million ($3 million
today) at auction in 1983.

WHERE?
THE LAST FACTORY,
MADISON AVENUE, BETWEEN 32ND AND 33RD STREETS, MANHATTAN.

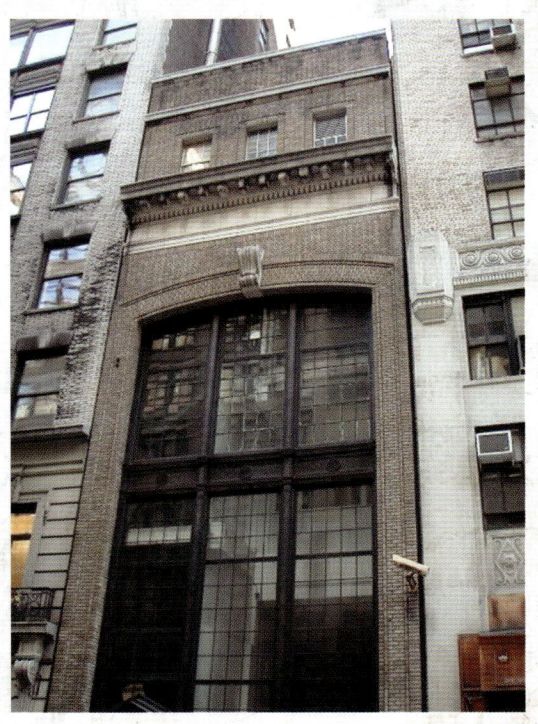

12

CARBONDALE, CO.

"All the women too ugly for portraits."
Andy Warhol on Colorado

It was John and Kimiko Powers, uber collectors of pop art, who introduced Andy to their neck of the woods in Colorado, 30 miles outside Aspen. In addition to Lichtenstein, Rauschenberg, Oldenburg, Jasper Johns and, later, Christo (who draped a valley for them), they became avid collectors of Warhol. They bought a *200 Soup Cans*, 10 *Marilyns*, 10 *Electric Chairs*, 10 *Flowers* and 10 *Maos*. Warhol also did a screenprint portrait of Kimiko. Something in the Colorado landscape spoke to Warhol: he bought 40 acres near the Powers' place, and helped them establish a modern art museum at Colorado State University, though in typically waspish fashion, Warhol was not too impressed by some of the locals at the private views. The Powers' American pop art collection became one of the most comprehensive in the World, touring frequently after Andy's death. In 2014, the collection was permanently housed in the elegant, understated, Powers Art Center, Carbondale.

WHERE?
THE ROCKIES AT CARBONDALE,
NEAR DENVER,
COLORADO.

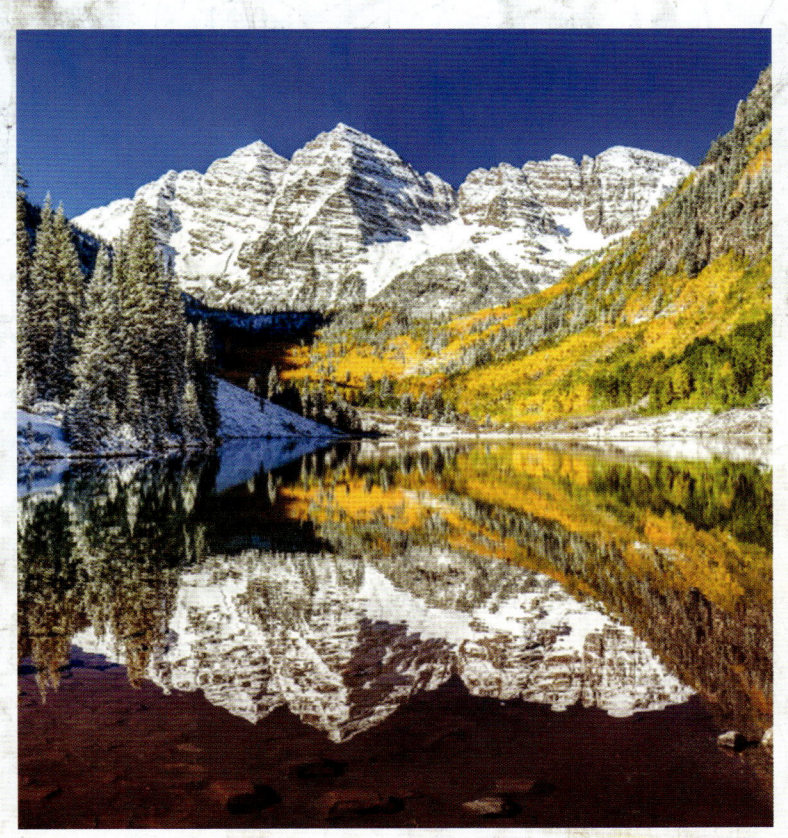

13

BASQUIAT

"Jean-Michel gave Andy a rebellious image again." Ronnie Cutrone

From a young age Basquiat had completely idolised Warhol. Aged 17, he even interrupted him once having lunch in a restaurant, and sold Andy a postcard of his work. Later, Basquiat kept trying to get access to the Factory, without success. Warhol, who didn't like poor black drug addicts (Warhol's default racism was well documented), gave his team the simple instruction "Don't let Jean-Michel in." But Basquiat was starting to get noticed, and was then taken up by art dealer Annina Nosei and, in Europe, by Bruno Bischofberger. When Andy discovered that Basquiats were being sold for $20,000, he changed his tune. Bruno had recognised that Warhol was getting boring and suggested a collaboration. Andy rented Basquiat his Great Jones Street loft, they worked out together at the gym and hung out at clubs; Andy wore cool clothes again. But the show of their work, at the Shafrazi Gallery in 1985, was panned. Basquiat was devastated. Warhol, his image burnished by Basquiat's druggy cool, moved on. Basquiat felt used and never really recovered, descending deeper into his addictions. He died in Andy's loft from an overdose in 1988, aged 27.

WHERE?
ANDY AND JEAN-MICHEL BASQUIAT AT THE SHAFRAZI
GALLERY OPENING OF THEIR SHOW, 1985.

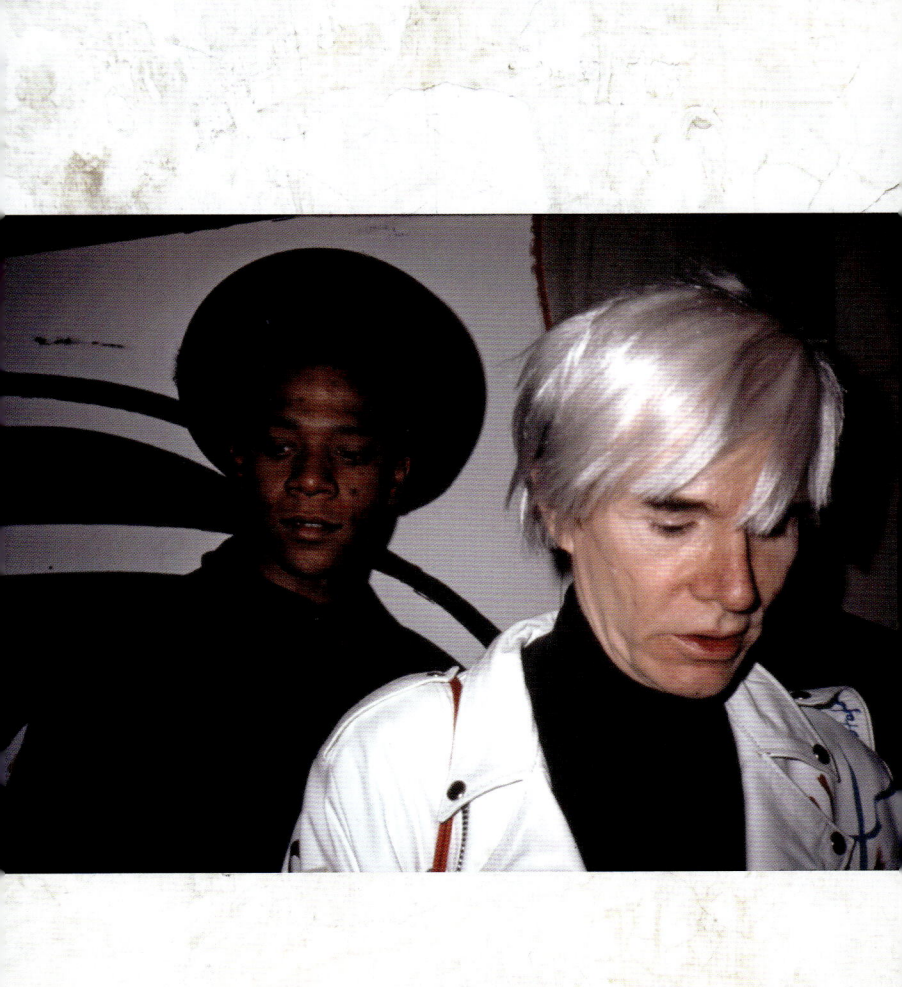

14

THE SOUP KITCHEN

"...an environment where no one knew who he was, and he just loved it."
Wilfredo Rosado

Andy hated Christmas, Easter and Thanksgiving. It interrupted the flow of work and his routine, to which he had become addicted. He was not interested in travel for travel's sake. The idea of exploring and soaking up a new place bored him stiff. He just didn't see the point. His clever head of publicity at *Interview*, Paige Powell, would therefore arrange for him to serve the homeless at soup kitchens at the Church of the Holy Redeemer on each of these holidays. Andy was surprisingly good at it, even bringing along tin foil so he could wrap supplies for those who needed to take something home. He loved talking to the old ladies who came to the soup kitchens – they reminded him of Julia, he said. This was another facet of Catholic Andy, reconnecting with his poor Slovakian background. It was almost a diarised dose of reality, akin to his going to church as a way to refresh, before he launched back into the brittle, facile worlds of celebrity, parties and the endless social climbing nature of Manhattan society.

WHERE?
THE CHURCH OF THE HOLY REDEEMER,
LOWER EAST SIDE,
MANHATTAN.

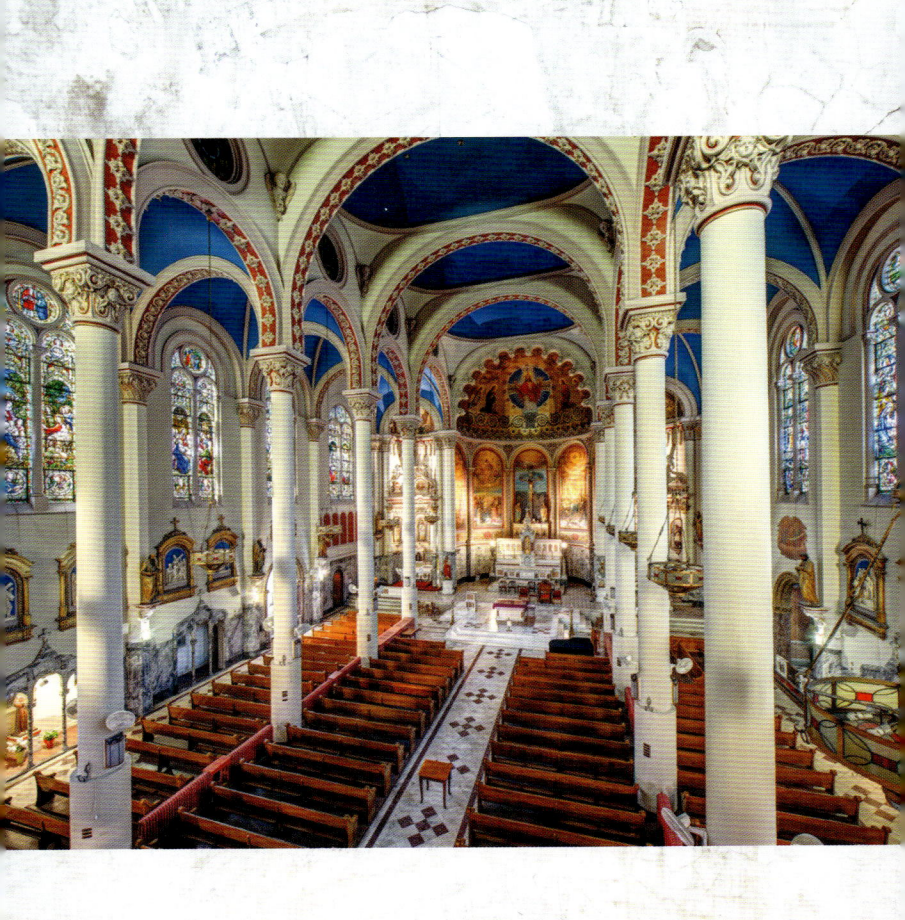

ANTHONY D'OFFAY

"As a painter of portraits, Warhol had no equal in...perhaps all of the 20th Century."
Anthony d'Offay, mega art dealer.

D'Offay was London's most influential dealer in modern art in the 1980s. It was he who had first shown Beuys and it was at Beuys's house in Naples, where d'Offay saw a 6 ft x 5 ft portrait by Andy in a bedroom, that an idea gelled: Warhol should do a show of self-portraits. Andy came for the opening on July 8th, 1986. He played the press wonderfully, stating that he was doing self-portraits as "I've kinda run out of money" or, "I've kinda run out of ideas." Andy adored London and d'Offay put him up in a suite at the Ritz. There were dinners at Mr Chow and a big dinner at Brown's Hotel for 120 to celebrate the show. It was a triumph and Andy returned to New York happy, with a commission from d'Offay to do a big portrait of Samuel Beckett. Andy's reputation was once more on the up, and in the second half of '86 he began working on his *Last Supper* paintings – planned for Milan in '87 – and a set of Lenin portraits for a show in Munich the same year.

WHERE?
ANDY PHOTOGRAPHED AT
THE ANTHONY D'OFFAY GALLERY IN 1986.

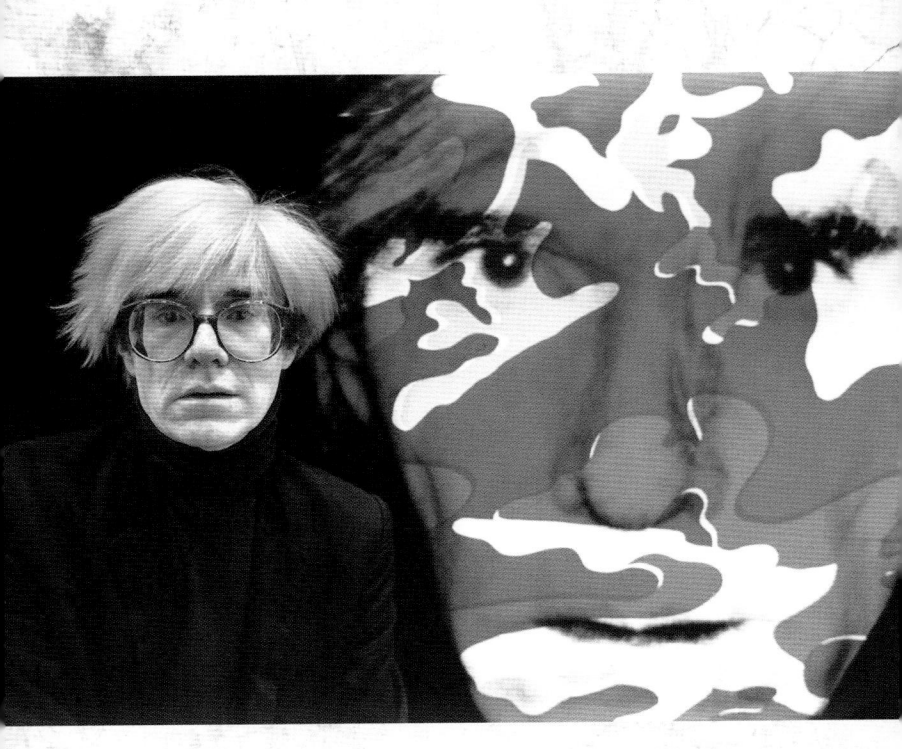

16

HEAVEN AND HELL ARE JUST ONE BREATH AWAY

Andy had a heightened, superstitious awareness of death, as the title above, from one of his *Last Supper* paintings, suggests. Andy never went to funerals, not even Julia's. When Factory members were reported to have died, he didn't react or register the fact. The Warholas had a history of gall bladder problems. Andy's dad had his removed aged 39 and Andy's began to be troublesome when he turned 43. Such was his fear of hospitals, that he did nothing about it. It was the Shah's surgeon who, following Andy declaring he had been in major pain since the beginning of 1987, told him he needed surgery immediately. Andy was admitted to New York Hospital on Thursday February 19th, with the op scheduled for Saturday. He told Paige Powell not to cancel tickets to the ballet on Sunday. In normal circumstances, this op is routine, but Andy's gall bladder was found to be full of gangrene. Yet all seemed to go OK. That Saturday evening Andy was in his room making calls. At 4am on Sunday morning his nurse checked on him asleep; all seemed fine. But a second check, at 6am, led to panic. Andy had turned blue and was unresponsive. Resuscitation efforts failed. The king of pop art was dead. Ventricular fibrillation was the cause. Andy's heart had stopped.

WHAT?
SHAMELESS NEW YORK PRESS:
ANDY'S DEATH JUXTAPOSED WITH MICK AND JERRY GETTING MARRIED.
ANDY WOULD HAVE APPRECIATED HOW FACILE THIS FRONT PAGE WAS.

NEW YORK POST

Monday February 23 1987   35 CENTS

METRO | SPORTS FINAL

TODAY: Snow, mid 30s.
TONIGHT: Clear, mid 30s.
TOMORROW: Sunny, mid 30s. Details: Page 2.

TV listings: P. 75

ANDY WARHOL DEAD AT 58

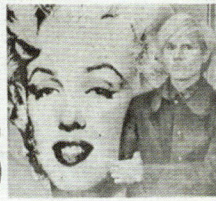

Prince of pop art who turned a soup can into museum treasure

● LIFE & TIMES OF A MEDIA GENIUS — SEE PAGES 4, 5 & 15

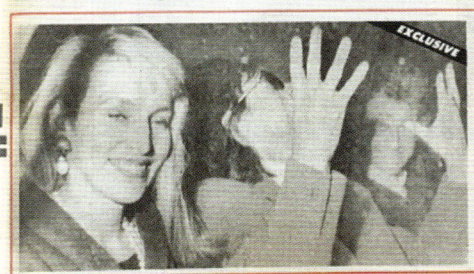

EXCLUSIVE

Jubilant Jagger 'n Jerry set the date — at last!

Mick's joyous gesture says it all as the couple leave Manhattan's Cafe Des Artistes yesterday after a brunch celebrating Jerry's acquittal in Barbados on drug charges. Her story of jail ordeal AND their wedding plans on PAGE 3

EXCLUSIVE photo Geoffrey Croft

HEART ATTACK KILLS DAVID SUSSKIND: PAGE 9

WARHOL RISING

Andy had his artistic breakthrough in 1960, when he painted his Coke bottles. But no one in the gallery world was really that interested. Leo Castelli rejected Andy for a show in 1961 but that same year Andy sold the perceptive Robert Scull, owner of a taxi company who was keen on art, six paintings for $1400 – just $233 each. In 1962 he created his *Soup Cans* and had a show that year at the Ferus gallery in L.A. The soup can paintings were available at $100 each. He eventually sold 32 as a set to the art dealer Irving Blum for $1000 – $31.25 each (Blum later sold the set to MOMA for a cool $15,000,000). By November 1962, things had perked up a little. At his Stable Gallery show Andy sold a Gold Marilyn for $800, but you could still buy regular Marilyns for $250. Amazingly many of his friends rejected gifts of paintings from Andy, telling others how they hated his work, or selling them on for a couple of hundred bucks. Things seemed to be going backwards when Andy created his *Death and Disaster* series. No gallery in New York would show them. A friend of Andy's refused one as a gift. Andy had warned his friends to hold onto his paintings as they would be worth something one day. It all fell on deaf ears. But the art market eventually took notice. Andy broke the record price for a living American artist in 1970, with his *Big Campbell's Soup Can*, which went for $70,000. Since then his rise has been stratospheric. How Andy must now be smiling wryly from his grave, but how do his friends, or their descendants, feel when they see this list of the recent sale prices of 15 of Andy's paintings from the early 1960s today? Can they bear to look?

$11,776,000
1962 *Small Torn Campbell's Soup Can*

$36,005,000
1962 *Four Marilyns*

$37,000,000
1963 *Double Elvis*

$38,245,000
1962 *Four Marilyns*

$38,442,500
1963 *Self Portrait*

$41,045,000
1962 *White Marilyn*

$43,762,500
1962 *Statue of Liberty*

$56,165,000
1963 *Mona Lisa*

$57,285,000
1962 *Coca Cola*

$63,362,500
1962 *Men in her Life*

$71,700,000
1962 *Turquoise Marilyn*

$81,925,000
1963 *Triple Elvis*

$100,000,000
1963 *Eight Elvises*

$105,400,000
1963 *Silver Car Crash (Double Disaster)*

And what about the prints? In 2019 Sotheby's sold one of an edition of 250 *Campbell's Soup 1*, for £783,000 ($1.2 million), valuing the complete edition at $300,000,000.

WHERE'S WARHOL TODAY?

It's telling that, amongst the endless celebrity and his projected personae, Warhol remained true to his roots. He stuck to his Ruthenian Catholic religion all his life and on his death two museums, Pittsburgh and Medzilaborce, would receive the bulk of his work. He had no desire to be entombed at MOMA. Luckily a few institutions around the world did buy and so have holdings. The relentless round of very popular Warhol exhibitions looks after the rest.

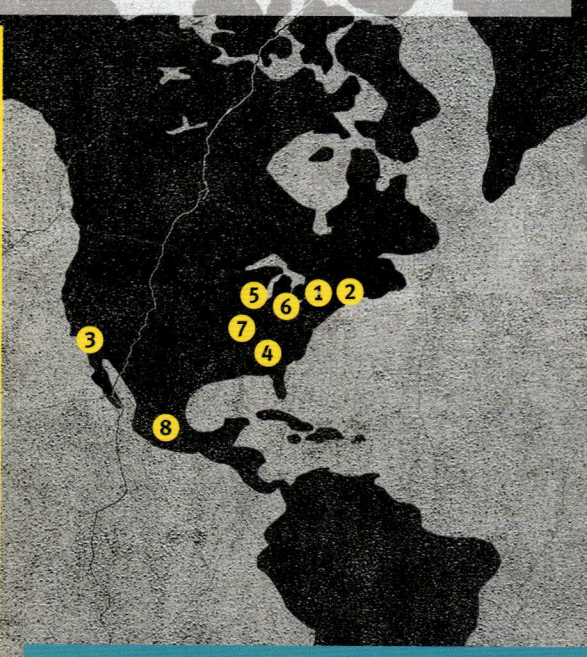

AMERICAS
Permanent collections

1. Pittsburgh
The Andy Warhol Museum. 900 paintings. 100 sculptures. 1000 prints. 4000 photographs. 610 time capsules. The world's biggest Warhol collection.

2. New York
MOMA. Over 100 works.

3. Los Angeles
The Broad. 26 Warhol masterpieces. MOCA. 14 works.

4. Atlanta
High Museum of Art. 23 works.

5. Chicago
Museum of Contemporary Art. 19 works.

6. Detroit
Detroit Institute of Arts.

7. Carbondale
Powers Art Centre.

8. Mexico City
Museo Jumex. Collection includes 100 Campbell's Soup Cans.

OTHER WARHOL EXHIBITIONS SINCE 2000:
Bilbao, Spain
Oxford, UK
Munich, Germany
Green Castle, IN
Williamstown, MD
Liverpool, UK
Chemnitz, Germany
Petersburg, Florida
Shanghai, China
Humblebaek, Denmark
French West Indies
Charlotte, NC
Milan, Italy
Amsterdam, Netherlands
Montreal, Canada
Oslo, Norway
Memphis, TN
Regina, Canada
Brisbane, Australia
Madrid, Spain
Prague, Czech Rep
Hiroshima, Japan
Taipei, Taiwan
Toledo, Ohio
Sao Paulo, Brazil

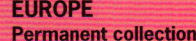

MAJOR WARHOL EXHIBITIONS SINCE 2000

Los Angeles, MOCA, 2002
London, Hayward Gallery, 2008
Paris, Grand Palais, 2009
New York, MOMA, 2010
New York, Brooklyn Museum, 2010
New York, The Met, 2012
Paris, MAM, 2015
New York, Whitney, 2018
London, Tate, 2020

EUROPE
Permanent collections

1. London
Saatchi Gallery
National Portrait Gallery
Tate Modern

2. Edinburgh
Scottish National Gallery

3. Berlin
Hamburger Bahnhof
Museum of Contemporary Art

4. Frankfurt
Museum für Moderne Kunst. Includes part of the Ströher collection.

5. Medzilaborce, Slovakia
Andy Warhol Museum of Modern Art. The world's second biggest Warhol collection.

6. Paris
National Museum of Modern Art (Centre Georges Pompidou)

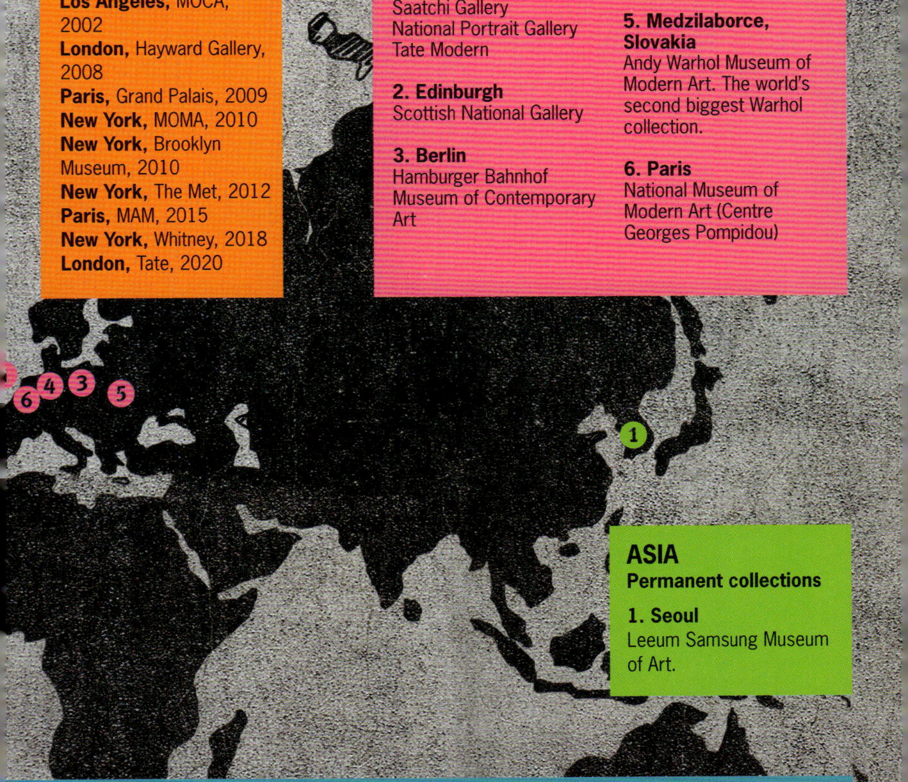

ASIA
Permanent collections

1. Seoul
Leeum Samsung Museum of Art.

Cologne, Germany	**Belgrade,** Serbia	**Wellington,** New Zealand	**Santiago,** Chile
Lyon, France	**Stockholm,** Sweden	**Haarlem,** Netherlands	**Manchester,** UK
Salzburg, Austria	**Tokyo,** Japan	**Marseilles,** France	**Edmonton,** Canada
Houston, TX	**Sydney,** Australia	**Salt Lake City,** UT	**Potsdam,** Germany
Monaco, France	**Omaha,** Nebraska	**Las Vegas,** NV	**Anchorage,** Alaska
Zurich, Switzerland	**St Kilda,** Australia	**Hong Kong**	**Indianapolis,** IN
Hamburg, Germany	**Seattle,** USA	**Krakow,** Poland	**Lisbon,** Portugal
Basel, Switzerland	**Mons,** Belgium	**Zaragoza,** Spain	**San Francisco,** CA
Tel Aviv, Israel	**Rome,** Italy	**Aosta,** Italy	**Ottawa,** Canada
Knokke, Belgium	**Beijing,** China	**Washington DC**	**Bogota,** Colombia
Budapest, Hungary	**Baku,** Azerbaijan		**Rio,** Brazil

CREDITS

Photo credits below are listed in section and page title order. Graffito wishes to thank all individuals and picture libraries who helped track down sometimes elusive images.
In credits below, Alamy = Alamy Stock Photo.

BEGINNINGS
Mikova Alamy
3252 Dawson St Alamy
St Vitus's Dance Alamy
Carnegie Institute Alamy
Lower East Side Alamy
Chelsea and Upper West Side Alamy
Capote Alamy
216 E75th St Rex Features
The Hugo Gallery F. Huygen
The Plaza Hotel B. Cendrars
Serendipity Alamy
New York Public Library Alamy
I.Miller Alamy
Angkor Wat Alamy

1956-1963
Bodley Gallery Alamy
1342 Lexington Av Getty Images
Coke Rex Features
Geldzahler Rex Features
Campbell's Soup Alamy
Marilyn Rex Features
The Stable Gallery Alamy
The Firehouse B. Cendrars
Route 66 Alamy

1963-1969
The Factory No 1 Alamy
The Assembly Line Alamy
Empire Alamy
Leo Castelli Getty Images
Edie Rex Features
Paris Alamy
The Exploding Plastic Inevitable Getty Images

The Chelsea Hotel Alamy
Max's Kansas City Alamy
The Nude Restaurant Alamy
Arizona Alamy
The Factory 2 Alamy
The Shooting Alamy
The E.R. Getty Images

1969-1971
Esquire Alamy
Fred Hughes Alamy
Hollywood 2 Alamy
Andy Warhol Enterprises Alamy
London Alamy
Munich Alamy
London: Pork Alamy
Bowie and Jagger Getty Images
Eothen, Montauk Alamy
Mao Zedong Alamy
St Moritz Alamy
Paris 2 Rex Features
Cinecittà Alamy
Interview Getty Images

1974-1987
Factory No 3 Rex Features
The Halston House Alamy
57 East 66th St Alamy
Chadds Ford Alamy
Teheran Alamy
Studio 54 Alamy
The White House Alamy
The Mudd Club Alamy
Andy Warhol TV Alamy
St Vincent Ferrer Alamy
The Anvil Alamy
The Factory 4 Alamy

Carbondale Alamy
Basquiat Alamy
The Soup Kitchen Fr. Gilbert Brown
Heaven and Hell Alamy

Andy Warhol illustration on cover: Gilly Lovegrove

This is an unauthorised publication. The contents, analysis and interpretations within express the views and opinions of Graffito Books Ltd only. All images in this book have been produced with the knowledge and prior consent of the picture libraries and photographers concerned.

Art Director:
Karen Wilks
Managing Editor:
Anthony Bland
Copy & Research Editor:
Serena Pethick

A note on the author:
Of Anglo-Spanish parentage, Ian Castello-Cortes grew up in South America and Cambridge, England. He is a publisher and writer with a particular interest in contemporary art and counter-cultures. Ian studied Modern History at Oxford University.

First published in the United States of America by Gingko Press, March 2020.
Gingko Press, Inc.: 2332 Fourth Street, Suite E, Berkeley, CA 94710, USA.
Gingko Press Verlags GmbH: Schulterblatt 58, 20357 Hamburg, Germany.
Published under license from Graffito Books, UK
© Graffito Books Ltd, 2020. www.graffitobooks.com
ISBN: 978-1-584237242 All rights reserved.
Printed in China.